G000253360

Crochet

Ann Stearns teaches fashion at the Oxford College of Further Education. She has written a book on Macramé for fashion and has contributed to the Marshall Cavendish publication *Fashion Maker*.

Scalloped border of Irish crochet, late nineteenth century

Crochet
Ann Stearns

Pan Original Pan Books London and Sydney

First published 1979 by Pan Books Ltd,
Cavaye Place, London SW10 9PG
©Ann Stearns 1979
ISBN 0 330 25840 0
Printed in Great Britain by
Butler & Tanner Ltd, Frome, Somerset

Also in the Pan Craft Book series

Needlework
Candlemaking
Filography
Creative patchwork
Jewellery
Pottery
Country crafts
Brass rubbing
Macramé
Machine knitting
Appliqué
Framing
Soft toys
More soft toys
Creative flowermaking
The art of dried and pressed flowers
Rugmaking
Weaving
Leatherwork

Contents

Acknowledgements
Introduction
Abbreviations

1 **Materials and equipment**

2 **Primary stitches**
  Slip loop
  Chain stitch
  Slip stitch
  Double chain
  Double crochet
  Half treble
  Treble stitch
  Additional stitches

  to make Pocket scarf
           Neck purses
           Tote bag

3 **Increasing and decreasing**
  Single stitches
  More than one stitch
  To neaten a shaped edge

  to make Petal choker

4 **Five crochet stitches to practise**
  Counterpane stitch
  Ridged double crochet
  Trebles in relief
  Raised trebles
  Raised crossed double trebles

  to make bag using three stitches
           bag using two stitches

5 **More advanced stitches**
  Check stitch
  Step stitch
  Crossed double trebles
  Surface zig-zag stitch
  Broom-handle stitch
  Star stitch
  One-way star stitch
  Horizontal trebles
  Shell stitch
  Bullion stitch

  to make Cushion using check stitch

6 **Open stitches**
  Chain lace
  Spaced trebles
  Crossed trebles
  Trebles and looped chain
  Solomon's knot stitch

  to make Beach bags
           Vegetable bag
           Scarf/stole
           Hat

7 Textured effects

Loop stitch
Cluster or pine stitch
Bobble stitch
Chain fur stitch
Cut fur stitch
Popcorn stitch
Block stitch
Accordion stitch
Multiple loop stitch

to make Two textured cushions
Scarf using accordion stitch
Hat using accordion stitch
Coat using accordion stitch
Waistcoat using multiple loop stitch

8 Crochet stitches using colour for effect

Chevron stitch
Zig-zag stitch
Woven fabrics
Stitches using colour to form stripes

to make House boots in chevron stitch
Jacket in three colours
Evening bag using woven fabrics
Leg warmers using stripes
Jumper using stripes
Two belts using woven fabrics

9 Filet crochet

Basic stitches
Blocks and spaces
Chart designing

to make Black shawl
Scarf

10 Fabrics

Circles and squares
Crazy patchwork
Geometric patchwork

to make Evening bag
Evening skirt
Jacket
Cushion

11 Working methods

Reading patterns
Tension
Pressing and blocking
Joining your work
Joining yarn
Finishing touches: cords, tassels and fringes
Designing your own fashion outfits

12 Experimental crochet

Rag rugs
Crochet over string and cord
Crochet over layers of yarn to form a circle
Crochet over a string mesh
Crochet using leather pieces
Surface crochet

to make Rag rug with pile effect
Rug
Two belts
Bolero
Gold leather belt
Leather bag
Tote bag

Index

Acknowledgements

My thanks are due to Iris Campin who made up many of the designs in this book, working from a calico toile, and for patiently checking all the instructions. Thanks are also due to Jean Leigh, who kindly lent me the shawl illustrated on page 50; to José Allan who supplied the fine piece of work on page 84; to Eina Argyle for the bag on page 10; and to my daughter Lucy who modelled many of the outfits in this book. Acknowledgement should also be made to the Victoria and Albert Museum, London, who gave permission to publish the photograph of Irish lace on page 2 and to Peter Murphy who took the photograph of the hat which is figure 116. Thanks to Patons and Baldwins Ltd; and to H. G. Twilley who supplied most of the yarns for the pieces I made especially for this book and Abel Morrall who supplied the hooks. Lastly my thanks are due to my husband Bryan who took the photographs and gave me help and encouragement during the writing of this book.
A.S.
Horton–cum–Studley

A little crochet bag made by a Korean girl of nine, during the 1920s
Various colours of cotton yarn are worked in ridged double crochet stitch

Introduction

Whilst crochet is one of the simplest crafts to learn, it is nevertheless capable of use in a wider spectrum of creative textile work than almost any other. And it is the intention of this book to illustrate its versatility both in range of work and imaginative application.

The origins of crochet are rather obscure but the craft is known to have been introduced into Europe during the sixteenth century. It flowered in the nineteenth century with the development of Irish crochet which classically imitates the Venetian needlemade laces. It is undeniable that the skill of the workers who produced this lace reach extraordinary levels of technique and artistry.

Crochet has been used in the designs of top couturiers for many years and can still be seen in many of the major collections, demonstrating the possibilities in high fashion of what is often thought of as a mere simple, homely craft.

The early chapters of this book illustrate in detail the basic stitches (which are fairly easy to master) and provide information concerning materials and equipment, both of which are cheap and easily obtained.

Whilst detailed instructions are provided for working a number of the designs illustrated (and it is recommended that some of these should be worked to develop techniques) I hope that you will be encouraged to produce your own designs, as this is clearly more rewarding than copying existing work. However, whilst complete instructions are not provided for the more complicated and advanced articles, information is given on how various effects may be achieved and methods for working out designs are suggested.

Abbreviations

ch	chain	
dc	double crochet	(USA single crochet)
h tr	half treble	(USA half double crochet)
tr	treble	(USA double crochet)
d tr	double treble	(USA treble)
tr tr	triple treble	(USA double treble)
quad tr	quadruple treble	(USA triple treble)

sl st	slip stitch
st(s)	stitch(es)
inc	increase
dec	decrease
yoh	yarn over hook

1 Materials and equipment

Materials suitable for crochet fall into two basic categories – natural and man-made. Natural yarns consist of wool, cotton, linen and silk, while the man-made yarns cover the rayon, acetate and plastic varieties. All manufacturers state the content on the wrapping and these should be read before purchasing. Sometimes natural and man-made yarns are mixed together and the properties of the yarn will be those of the higher proportion. It is important to read the manufacturer's instructions before you choose your yarn, to make sure the yarn is suitable for the purpose; that it will stand up to the wear expected, be comfortable, not stretch excessively, nor be affected by sunlight, and will wash.

Throughout this book all crochet material being used will be referred to as *yarn* – this should avoid confusion between the many different materials and threads now available. However, it cannot be stressed too strongly that the right choice of yarn will make or mar the success of your work. Always try out a sample run before starting a large piece of work to see the overall effect.

Choosing yarns is fun as there are so many available. When working a chosen commercial pattern you are strongly advised to use the yarn recommended. However, it is hoped that this book will encourage you to experiment with making up your own designs and choosing your own yarns. Points to watch when experimenting:

1 Complex crochet stitches look best in plain yarns.
2 Fancy yarns such as bouclé and crimped, and very fluffy yarns look best made up in more simple stitches and designs.
3 Contrasting yarns – smooth and hairy, shiny and matt, add interest to a sectioned design.
4 Hairy and textured yarns look best made up in very simple stitches. Little or no pattern in stitch or design would be seen if worked in a highly textured yarn.

Remember, also, that unconventional yarns can be used to advantage, for example string, raffia , parcel twine, ribbon, russia braid, etc.

Other materials can be incorporated with crochet, for instance leather and beads, as will be seen later in this book.

Having selected the yarn required for your work, the crochet hook must be chosen to give the correct tension to your work. Figure 1 shows the relationship between hook size and yarn thickness. Hooks are available from size 0·60mm to 10·00mm. All the usual yarns are illustrated showing the appropriate hook size. Crochet hook sizes are now standardized and will be quoted in the International Size Range (ISR) throughout this book.

Hook sizes and appropriate yarn

00·60mm	Coats' sewing thread
00·75mm	
1·00mm	Coats' number 50 Mercer crochet yarn
1·25mm	
1·50mm	Twilley's Twenty
1·75mm	
2·00mm	Twilley's Lyscorder
2·50mm	
3·00mm	3-ply yarn
3·50mm	
4·00mm	4-ply yarn
4·50mm	
5·00mm	Aran yarn
5·50mm	
6·00mm	Robin Flamingo chunky yarn
7·00mm	
8·00mm	Fancy yarn – textured
9·00mm	
10·00mm	Rug wool

Always select the right size hook for the yarn – usually a firm fabric is required with a regular tension – closeness of stitches. If your work is too loose it will lose shape quickly and become displeasing. Unusual and interesting effects can be obtained by using large hooks for fine yarns and vice versa, but this would be for the more experienced worker.

A tape measure, scissors, pressing tools, pins and the usual sewing equipment should all be to hand while working.

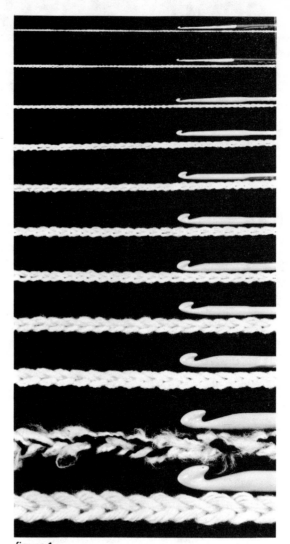

figure 1

2 Primary stitches

In order to master the stitches described in this chapter, it is advisable to select a large hook size and appropriate yarn, eg hook size number 4·50 ISR and a double knitting yarn, and practise each step as it is explained.

For the right-handed worker (the left-handed person should place the illustrations in front of a mirror to obtain the reversed image), hold the yarn with the left hand (figure 2) and the hook in the right hand (figure 3). Note that the yarn should be wrapped around the fingers of the left hand, and this will control the flow of yarn. The third and fourth fingers should be well together and the yarn placed over the fourth finger.

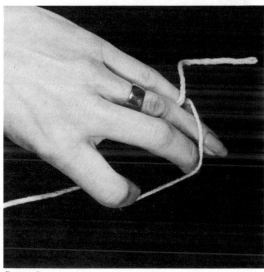

figure 2

figure 3

figure 4

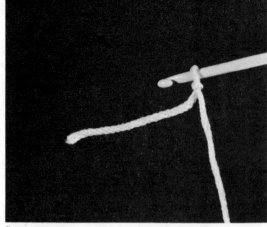

figure 5

Slip loop

The slip loop is made by twisting the yarn from the ball as shown in the photograph and placing the hook into this loop (figures 4 and 5). This will form the first stitch on your hook and will enable you to start a foundation chain length. Draw the yarn tightly over the hook and with the left hand hold the cut end of yarn between the thumb and the first finger. Place the yarn from behind the hook over the fingers of the left hand (figure 6). Now you are ready to start your first chain length.

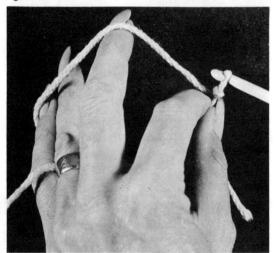

figure 6

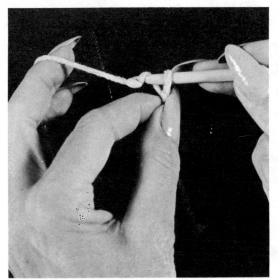

figure 7

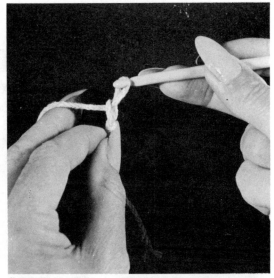

figure 8

Chain stitch (ch)

It is important to hold the cut end of yarn immediately under the hook between the thumb and the first finger of the left hand whilst working most stitches. To work the chain stitch, which is the foundation of most crochet work, take the hook in front of the yarn which passes over and between the first and second fingers of the left hand and place the hook under the yarn. This is known as *yarn over hook* and will be abbreviated to *yoh* (figure 7). Draw the yarn through the loop on the hook. One chain stitch has been worked, ie 1 ch (figure 8). Repeat until the required length of chain is complete. Figure 9 illustrates the working of a chain length. Practise this stitch until a chain length formed with even-sized stitches is mastered. Note that the slip loop does not count as a chain stitch when working to a given number of stitches. Figure 10 illustrates three chain lengths:

(a) a poor, uneven length of chain
(b) a good, well-formed, even length of chain
(c) the reverse side of (b).

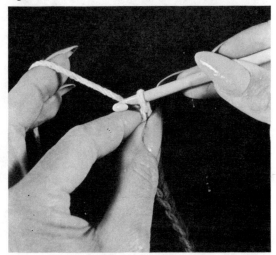

figure 9

figure 10

figure 11

Slip stitch (sl st)

This is the smallest crochet stitch worked. It is used to move the working stitch to the required position when working a shaped area. To work slip stitch: complete a length of chain to form the foundation, eg 10 chain stitches. Miss the last chain stitch worked and insert the hook into the next stitch (figure 11). The thumb indicates the position. Place yarn over the hook as shown in figure 12 and draw the yarn through the chain stitch and through the stitch on the hook (figure 13). One slip stitch has been worked. Repeat to end of chain.

The hook may be placed in any part of the foundation chain, ie the back top single loop (figure 14), or both top loops of the chain (figure 15), or the two top loops (figure 16), or the single loop on the reverse side of the chain (figure 17). Select whichever method you find the easiest, but it is important that a consistent stitch is made, and the same method should be used throughout the same piece of work. This applies to all crochet work.

Some people prefer to use a larger hook size when working the foundation chain, changing to a smaller hook size for the following rows. The larger hook gives a slacker chain stitch, thus allowing the hook to enter each stitch more easily on the following row.

To end work When a length of crochet is complete, the working stitch on your hook should be secured firmly. To do this, simply draw the yarn through the last stitch on the hook and cut the yarn leaving an end of 4in (10cm). Pull the cut end tightly (figure 18).

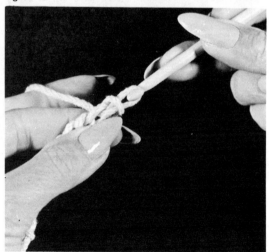

figure 12

figure 13

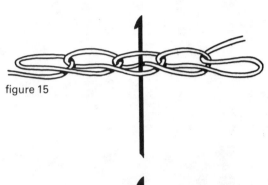

figure 14

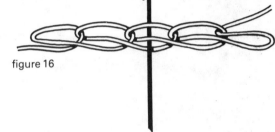

figure 15

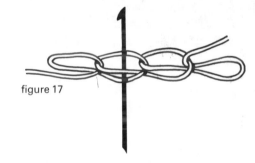

figure 16

figure 17

figure 18   pull tightly →

Double chain (d ch)

This is an alternative method of working a foundation chain which many people find easier to work. To work a double chain, make 2 chains, place the hook under one loop of the first chain worked, place yarn over hook (figure 19) and draw yarn through (2 loops on hook) (figure 20). Place yarn over hook (figure 21) and draw through both loops on hook (figure 22).

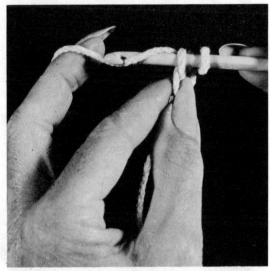

figure 19

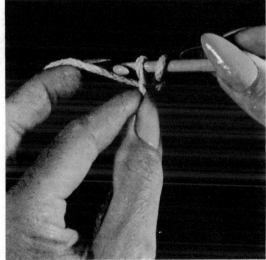

figure 20

19

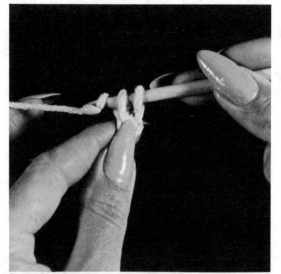

figure 21

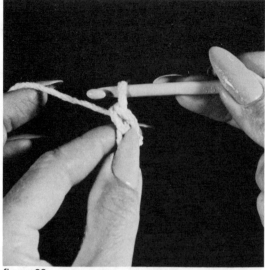

figure 22

figure 23

figure 24

Continue working in this manner placing the hook in the single left loop (figure 23), yarn over hook and draw through yarn (2 loops on hook). Place yarn over hook and draw through both loops on hook (figure 24).

This makes a firm foundation and is also useful for a tying cord or belt if it is worked in a really thick yarn.

Double crochet (dc)

When the foundation stitches are mastered you can start to work a fabric – the first stitch to learn is double crochet. As crochet is formed with one stitch on the hook and as this stitch is always on the top edge of your work, turning chains have to be added when working dc because this stitch has more depth than slip stitch. Turning chains lift the working stitch to the required position before starting your new row. The number of turning chains varies according to the stitch and the table on page 23 gives the details. For double crochet, one chain is required as a turning chain. Therefore, to give a length of work consisting of 10 stitches, 11 chain stitches should be worked for the foundation. Place hook into the third chain from hook (figure 25). Place yarn over hook (figure 26) and draw through yarn (two loops on hook) (figure 27). Yarn over hook (figure 28) and draw through both loops on hook (figure 29). One double crochet has been worked, ie 1 dc. Continue to work 1 dc into each ch stitch to end of foundation chain.

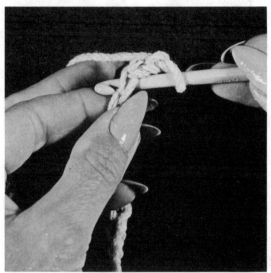

figure 25

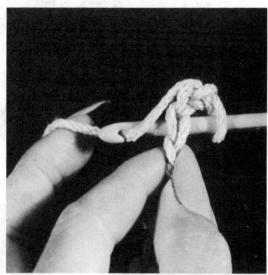

figure 26

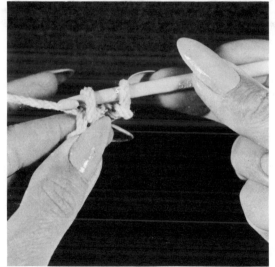

figure 27

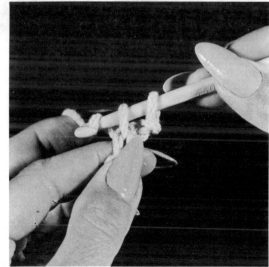

figure 28

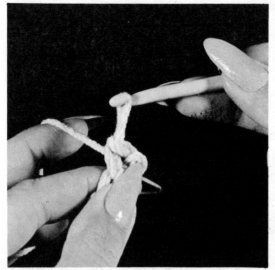
figure 29

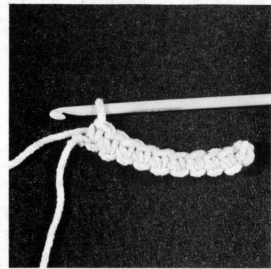
figure 30

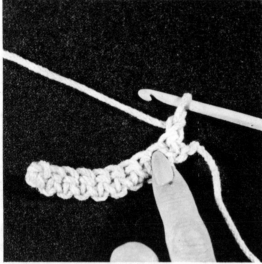
figure 31

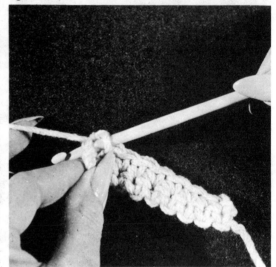
figure 32

Figure 30 shows 9 dc plus the turning chain at the start of the row, ie 10 sts. Turn your work and start the next row.

Figure 31 illustrates the turning chain worked at the start of the row and the position for working the first dc, ie the hook is placed into the third stitch from the hook. Always place the hook under both loops of the previous row unless stated otherwise. The last dc should be worked into the turning chain of the previous row (figure 32).

The table below lists for each stitch the additional chains required to count as the first stitch of the first row, on a foundation chain; the position for placing the first stitch of the first row; the number of turning chains required at the start of a new row; the position for placing the last stitch of each row and the position for placing the first stitch for each additional new row.

The additional chains required on a foundation chain, and the turning chains for each stitch

Stitch required. Yarn over hook ( ) times	Additional chains to foundation★	First stitch placed into:	Number of turning chains	Last stitch of each row placed into:	For following rows, first stitch is placed into:
slip stitch	1	second chain from hook			
double crochet	1	third chain from hook	1	first chain of turning chain	third stitch from hook
half treble (1)	2	fourth chain from hook	2	second chain of turning chain	fourth stitch from hook
treble (1)	3	fifth chain from hook	3	third chain of turning chain	fifth stitch from hook
double treble (2)	4	sixth chain from hook	4	fourth chain of turning chain	sixth stitch from hook
triple treble (3)	5	seventh chain from hook	5	fifth chain of turning chain	seventh stitch from hook
quadruple treble (4)	6	eighth chain from hook	6	sixth chain of turning chain	eighth stitch from hook

★ to count as first pattern stitch of first row

For most crochet techniques, your work is turned for each new row. However, variations can be achieved by working 'one-way' crochet, ie by having a definite right and wrong side to your work. To do this, the yarn has to be broken at the end of each row, and rejoined at the start of each new row. The work is therefore *not* turned at the end of the row. The same effect is also achieved when working in continuous circles.

Different patterns are also achieved by the hook placement, ie under the single back loop of the stitch of the previous row, or the single front loop of the stitch of the previous row, or *both* loops of the stitch of the previous row – this is the most usual method. There are other techniques also, which will be illustrated later in the book.

Figure 33 illustrates a completed sample of dc.

Note: always turn the work in the same direction to give a firm, even edge.

Most crochet techniques are turned at the end of each row, and worked to and fro, making the work reversible. However, in the various techniques covered in this book, there are exceptions and special comment will be made.

The turning chains are always worked at the start of the new row. When working your first *square* sample, count your stitches at the end of each row to make sure they remain constant.

Remember that the turning chain(s) should be counted as one stitch of the pattern.

Half treble (h tr)

Work a length of chain, eg 10 ch plus 2 ch to act as the turning chains for the first row. Place the yarn over hook *before* inserting hook into the fourth chain from hook (figure 34), place yarn over hook (figure 35) and draw through yarn (3 loops on hook) (figure 36). Place yarn over hook (figure 37) and draw through *all* loops on hook (figure 38), ie one half treble stitch has been worked – 1 h tr.

Figure 39 illustrates 9 half trebles completed and the turning chains worked at the start of the row, ie 10 stitches. Turn your work and start the next row.

Figure 40 illustrates the two turning chains worked, and the position is indicated for placing the hook for the first half treble (ie the fourth stitch from hook).

Figure 41 illustrates the second row complete. Note the last half treble is worked into the second chain of the turning chains.

Figure 42 shows the completed half treble sample.

figure 33

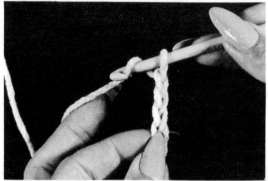

figure 34

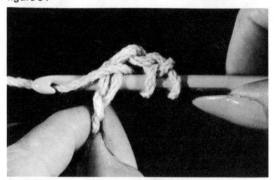

figure 35

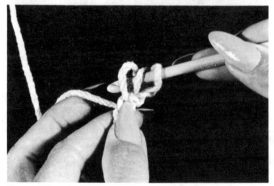

figure 36

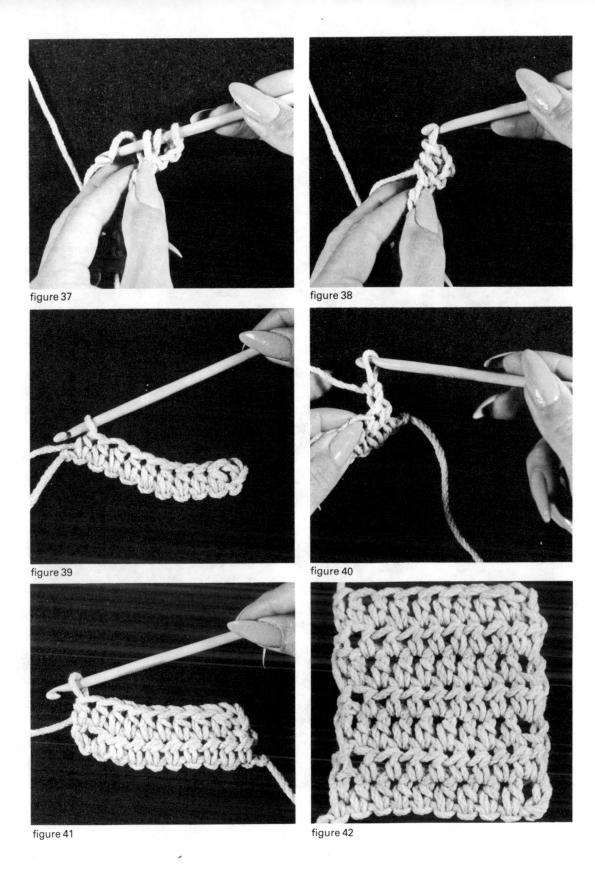

figure 37

figure 38

figure 39

figure 40

figure 41

figure 42

Treble stitch (tr)

Work a length of chain, eg 10 ch, plus 3 ch to act as the turning chains for the first row. Place yarn over hook before inserting the hook into the fifth chain from hook (figure 43). Place yarn over hook (figure 44) and draw through yarn (3 loops on hook) (figure 45). Place yarn over hook (figure 46) and draw through 2 loops (figure 47). Place yarn over hook (figure 48) and draw through 2 loops (figure 49). One treble stitch has been worked, ie 1 tr.

Figure 50 illustrates the completed row of 10 sts with the work turned and 3 turning chains worked for the start of the second row. The position is indicated for placing the hook for the first treble, ie the fifth stitch from hook.

Figure 51 illustrates the second treble row completed. Note that the last treble is worked into the third chain of the turning chains.

Figure 52 illustrates the completed treble sample.

figure 43

figure 44

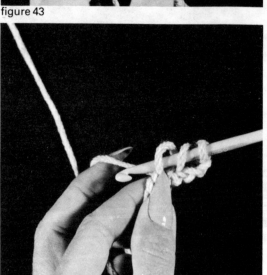

figure 45

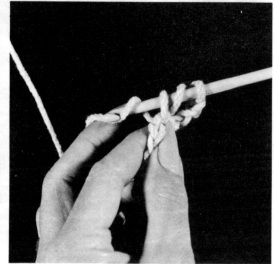

figure 46

figure 47

figure 48

figure 49

figure 50

figure 51

figure 52

Additional stitches

Double treble (d tr) is worked by placing yarn over hook twice (figure 53) before inserting the hook into the stitch of the previous row.

figure 53

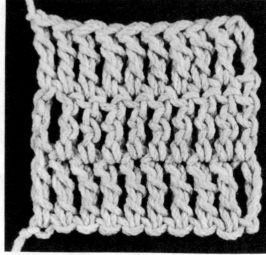

figure 54

Triple treble (tr tr) is worked by placing yarn over hook 3 times (figure 55) before inserting the hook into the stitch of the previous row, and

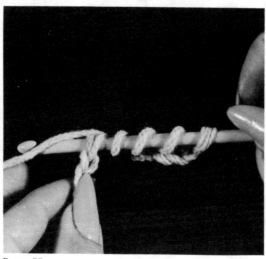

figure 55

figure 56

Quadruple treble (quad tr) yoh 4 times (figure 57). With each stitch, the yarn takes off 2 loops on the hook each time so each additional twist of yarn on the hook gives a greater stitch depth.

Figure 54 illustrates the completed sample of d tr, figure 56 of tr tr, and figure 58 of quad tr.

figure 57

figure 58

Neck purses   figure 59

1 ball of 25gm Twilley's Lyscordet or Lystwist. Number 2·50 ISR crochet hook.

Tension 6 dc and 5 rows to 1in (2·5cm)

Work a length of chain to give the required width for purse, eg 40 chain. Join with a slip stitch to the first chain to form a circle. Continue in double crochet, working 1 ch to start the new round and count as 1 dc. Mark the 1 ch with a safety pin to show the start of the round. When the round is complete slip stitch into the chain at the start of round and re-mark with the safety pin. Continue in rounds until the required depth is worked – 3½in (9cm). End work and secure yarn. Sew the base together and add fringe (see chapter 11). Attach cords to top edge. The cord is made by working the required length (for either neck or waist) in double chain. Tassels can be added and a button and loop should be sewn to the centre to form the fastening (see chapter 11). Various shapes and sizes can be worked using this simple technique.

figure 59

Tote bag figure 60

5×50gm balls of Paton's Capstan yarn.
Number 5·50 ISR crochet hook.

Tension 6 dc and 9 rows to 2in (5cm)

Work 2 squares in double crochet over 40 sts.
Place both pieces together and sew three sides,
add a fringe to the base. A twisted cord and
tassels (see chapter 11) complete the bag. A
contrasting yarn colour has been used in the
illustration for the cord and fringing. However,
one colour may be used for this. The cord is
sewn down both sides of the bag leaving the
tassel to hang freely from the base edge.

Pocket scarf

colour illustration p49

9×25gm balls of Paton's Trident DK yarn.
Number 4·50 ISR crochet hook.

Tension 9 tr and 4 rows to 2in (5cm)

Work in treble stitch throughout over 33 sts.
Continue in treble stitch until the required
length, eg 91in (232cm). Sew up each end to give
a pocket depth of 7½in (19cm). A fringe may be
added as illustrated, and a border edging in a
darker shade of yarn. (See chapter 11 for
working methods for fringe.)

figure 60

3 Increasing and decreasing

When the basic stitches are mastered it will be necessary to learn to shape your work by *increasing and decreasing*. Crochet work can be shaped either on the sides of the crochet or in the process of working a row. Both methods are described.

Increasing single stitches on the sides of your work It is neater to increase on the second stitch in from the edge and not on the outer stitch of your work. This will give a smoother line. To do this, simply work 2 sts into 1 st of the previous row – this applies to all the basic stitches covered in the last chapter.

Increasing stitches in the course of a row For increasing 1 st simply work 2 sts into the same st of the previous row. If more than a 1 st increase is required, work 3 sts into the same st or 2 sts into 2 adjacent sts. This applies to all the basic stitches covered in the last chapter.

Figure 61 illustrates a 1 st increase in dc.

Figure 62 illustrates a 1 st increase in tr.

figure 61

figure 62

figure 63

figure 64

figure 65

figure 66

Decreasing single stitches Again it is neater to decrease on the second st in from the edge of your work for side shaping by working over 2 stitches of the previous row. When decreasing in the course of a row, work to the position required and use the same technique.

Figures 63 and 64 illustrate the method of decreasing 1 st in dc.

Figures 65 and 66 illustrate the method of decreasing 1 st in tr.

Increasing more than one st on the sides of your work To increase at the beginning of a row, work the required number of chain stitches, plus the extra chains for 'turning chains' and continue in **pattern (chart, p23) for the number of chains** according to your stitch.

Figure 67 illustrates an increase of 6 dc.

Figure 68 illustrates an increase of 5 tr.

To increase more than one st at the end of a row To increase at the end of a row, cast-on chains plus the extra turning chains must be made at the

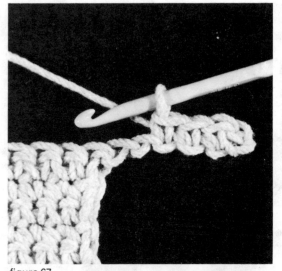

figure 67

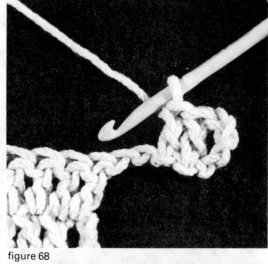

figure 68

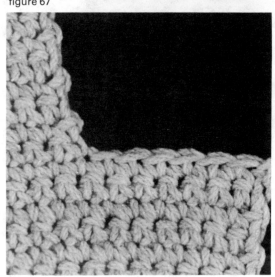

figure 69

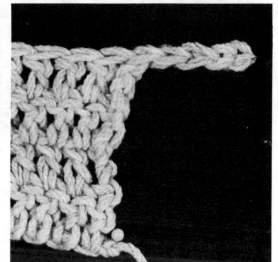

figure 70

beginning of the *previous* row to the row requiring the increase (chart, p23, shows number of chains according to your stitch). Slip stitch back along the cast-on chains the same number as the increase required; there will be some chains left unworked and these will be the turning chains to raise your working stitch. Complete row in pattern. On the return row, ie the increase row, work over the slip stitches giving the required stitch increase at the end of this row.

Figure 69 illustrates 4 sts increased in dc.

Figure 70 illustrates 4 sts increased in tr.

Decreasing more than one st at the sides of your work
To decrease at the start of a row, slip stitch over the number of sts for required decrease. Then work the right number of *turning chains* and continue in st required.

To decrease at the end of a row, count the number of sts to be decreased from the end of the row, place a safety pin in the st and work until you reach the st before the pin. Turn work and continue in st required.

33

figure 71

figure 72

To neaten a shaped edge Sometimes it is necessary to neaten and smooth the edge of your crochet where shaping has been worked, eg armholes and neck lines. Two methods are illustrated:

Figure 71 illustrates dc worked into each stitch of the row.

Figure 72 illustrates cord stitch which is dc worked from *left* to right.

Figure 73 illustrates the working of cord stitch in detail.

figure 73

Petal choker

5×25gm balls of Lystwist in 5 different shades – A, B, C, D, and E. Number 2·50 ISR crochet hook.

Tension 7 dc to 1in (2·5cm) and 8 rows to 1in (2·5cm).

Chain 111 for foundation chain in colour A.

Row 1 Work 1 dc into 3rd ch from hook. 1 dc in next 26 ch.

15 ch. Work 1 dc into 3rd ch from hook, 1 dc in next 12 ch.

1 dc in next 14 ch on foundation. 20 ch. Work 1 dc into 3rd ch from hook, 1 dc in next 17 ch. 1 dc in next 14 ch on foundation chain. 25 ch. Work 1 dc into 3rd ch from hook, 1 dc in next 22 ch. 1 dc in next 14 ch on foundation chain. 20 ch. Work 1 dc into 3rd ch from hook, 1 dc in next 17 ch. 1 dc in next 14 ch on foundation chain. 15 ch. Work 1 dc in 3rd ch from hook, 1 dc in next 12 ch. 1 dc in next 27 ch on foundation chain. Break off yarn and turn work.

Row 2 Join in colour B to 1st st. 1 ch. 1 dc into 3rd st from hook. 1 dc in next 24 dc. Dec. 1 st in next 2 dc at base of petal. 1 dc in next 12 dc. Increase 2 sts in next 2 dc (ie the tip of the petal). 1 dc in next 12 dc. Dec. 1st in next 2 dc. Continue working in dc increasing 2 sts on the tips of the petals and decreasing 1 st at the base of the petals to end of row. Break off yarn and turn work.

Row 3 Join in colour C to 1st st. Continue working in dc decreasing one st at the base of the petals, and working 1 increase st. 1 dc in next 2 sts, 1 increase st at the tips of the petals to end of row.

Row 4 Join in colour C to 1st st. Continue in colour C and work as last row increasing the number of single dc worked between the increased sts on the tips of the petals, and decreasing the number of single dc worked between the decreased sts at the base of the petals. Break off yarn and turn work.

Row 5 Join in colour D to 1st st. As row 4.

Row 6 Join in colour E to 1st st. As row 4.

Continue in this manner reversing the colour order.

When complete, add a hook and loop to the ends of the crochet to form the fastening.

The colour illustration (p49) shows a variation on this theme. This is achieved by working 3 half treble stitches for the increase stitches on the tips of the petals, with 3 half trebles worked into the centre stitch of the tip, on row 2, 3 and 6 and working 1 increased dc st over these positions on the following rows.

4 Five crochet stitches to practise

These stitches are shown in the two shoulder bags in figures 84 and 85. Practise the stitches with a Double Knitting yarn and a number 4·50 ISR crochet hook.

Counterpane stitch

figure 74

Make a chain length.

Row 1 2 ch to count as 1st stitch. Yoh and insert hook into fourth chain from hook. Yoh and draw through yarn and through 1 loop on hook. Yoh and draw through 2 loops on hook. One counterpane stitch has been worked. Repeat this stitch to end of chain. Turn work.

Row 2 2 ch to count as 1st st. 1 counterpane stitch in each stitch to end of row. 1 counterpane stitch in the 2nd chain of turning chains at end of row. Turn work. Repeat row 2 throughout.

This stitch forms a reversible fabric.

Figure 75 illustrates the working method of the stitch.

figure 74

figure 75

figure 76

figure 77

Ridged double crochet

figure 76

Make a chain length.

Work in double crochet stitch throughout but place the hook in the *back* loop of each stitch of the previous row. This gives the ridged effect.

This stitch forms a reversible fabric.

Figure 77 illustrates the working method of the stitch.

Trebles in relief

figure 78

Make a chain length.

figure 78

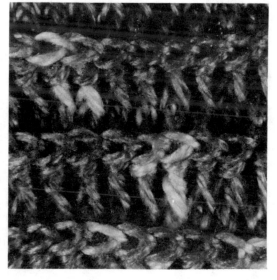

Row 1 3 ch to count as 1 tr. 1 tr in 4th chain from hook. 1 tr in each chain to end of row. Turn work.

Row 2 3 ch to count as 1 tr. Work next treble by placing the hook horizontally under the 2nd treble of last row. Yoh and draw through yarn (yoh and draw through 2 loops) twice. Repeat in each stitch to end of row. 1 tr in 3rd ch of turning chain. Turn work.

Repeat row 2 throughout.

This stitch forms a reversible fabric.

Figure 79 illustrates the working method of the stitch.

Colour illustration (p50) shows a hat worked in trebles in relief.

figure 79

Raised trebles figure 80

Make a chain length (even number).

Row 1 1 ch to count as 1st dc. 1 dc in 3rd ch from hook. 1 dc in each ch to end of row. Turn work.

Rows 2 and 3 1 ch to count as 1st dc. 1 dc in 3rd st from hook. 1 dc in each dc to end of row. Turn work.

Row 4 1 ch to count as 1st dc. 1 dc in 3rd st from hook. Yoh, miss last dc row and insert hook from right to left under 3rd dc of next row down (ie 2nd row down), yoh and draw through yarn (yoh and draw through 2 loops) twice – missing next dc of last row – 1 raised treble has been worked.

★ 1 dc in next st. Miss next dc of 2nd row down, 1 raised treble in next dc – missing next dc of last row. ★ Repeat from ★ to ★ to end of row. 1 dc in last st. Turn work.

figure 80

Row 5 As row 2.

Row 6 As row 4 working raised treble under the raised trebles of 2nd row down.

Rows 5 and 6 are repeated throughout.

There is a definite right and wrong side to this fabric.

Figure 81 illustrates the working method of the stitch.

figure 81

38

figure 82

figure 83

Raised crossed double trebles figure 82

Make a chain length – multiple of 3.

Row 1 1 ch to count as 1 dc. 1 dc in 3rd ch from hook. 1 dc in each ch to end of row. Turn work.

Row 2 3 ch to count as 1 tr. 1 tr in 5th st from hook. 1 tr in each st to end of row. Turn work.

Row 3 1 ch to count as 1 dc. 1 dc in 3rd st from hook. Yoh twice, insert hook under 1st tr from left to right, yoh and draw through yarn (yoh and draw through 2 loops) twice, yoh twice, miss 2 tr and insert hook under next tr from right to left, yoh and draw through yarn (yoh and draw through 2 loops) twice – 3 loops on hook. Insert hook into next dc of last row, yoh and draw through yarn, yoh and draw through all 4 loops on hook. 1 dc in next 2 sts. ★ Yoh twice, insert hook from left to right under same treble of last raised double treble, yoh and draw through yarn (yoh and draw through 2 loops) twice, yoh twice, miss 2 tr of last row, insert hook from right to left under next tr. Yoh and draw through yarn (yoh and draw through 2 loops) twice – 3 loops on hook. Insert hook into next dc of last row. Yoh and draw through loop. Yoh and draw through all 4 loops on hook. 1 dc in next 2 sts. ★ Repeat from ★ to ★ to end of row. Yoh twice, insert hook under same tr of last

raised double treble, yoh and draw through yarn (yoh and draw through 2 loops) twice. Insert hook into turning chain of previous row, yoh and draw through yarn, yoh and draw through all loops on hook. Turn work.

Row 4 3 ch to count as 1 tr. 1 tr in 5th st from hook. 1 tr in each st to end of row. Turn work.

Row 5 1 ch to count as 1 dc. Yoh twice, insert hook from right to left under 1st pair of double trebles. Yoh and draw through yarn (yoh and draw through 2 loops) twice. Insert hook into next dc. Yoh and draw through yarn, yoh and draw through all loops on hook. ★ 1 dc in next 2 sts. Yoh twice, insert hook from left to right under same pair of double trebles as last double treble worked, yoh and draw through yarn (yoh and draw through 2 loops) twice, yoh twice, insert hook from right to left under next pair of double trebles, yoh (figure 83) and draw through yarn (yoh and draw through 2 loops) twice. Insert hook into next dc of last row. Yoh and draw through yarn. Yoh and draw through all 4 loops on hook. ★ Repeat from ★ to ★ to end of row. 1 dc in turning chain.

Row 6 As row 4.

Rows 3, 4, 5, and 6 complete this pattern. There is a definite right and wrong side to this fabric.

The following patterns are for the two bags illustrated in figures 84 and 85.

39

figure 84

Bag using three stitches

figure 84

counterpane stitch
ridged double crochet
trebles in relief

Measurements 9in (23in) square (excluding the fringing). 8×25gm DK yarn. Number 5·50 ISR hook.

Tension 7 sts and 5 rows in counterpane st=2in (5cm).

Work 1 square over 30 sts in counterpane st.

Work 2 squares over 15 sts in ridged double crochet and trebles in relief (two in each st).

Join the four small squares together and make up the bag by joining three sides of the completed squares together. Add a loop and button or tassel on to the centre of the opening to form a fastening.

A fringe and cord with tassels has been added to complete the finishing of this bag (chapter 11 for details).

40

figure 85

Bag using two stitches

figure 85

raised trebles
raised crossed double trebles

Measurements 9in (23cm) square (excluding the fringing). 8×25gm DK yarn. Number 5·50 ISR hook.

Tension as for previous bag.

Work 1 square over 30 sts in each stitch. Make up as for first bag.

5 More advanced stitches

This chapter covers ten different crochet stitches, each giving distinctive patterned effects. All the patterns are worked in single colours, and some include the more unusual techniques. Practise these stitches using a Double Knitting yarn and a number 4·50 ISR crochet hook before starting the suggested articles at the end of this chapter.

Check stitch   figure 86

Make a chain length – multiple of 4+2 (eg 12+2=14).

Row 1 1 ch to count as 1 dc. 1 dc in 3rd chain from hook. 1 dc in each chain to end. Turn work.

Row 2 1 ch to count as 1 dc. Placing the hook into the back single loop for *all* following double crochet stitches, work 1 dc in 3rd stitch from hook, and 1 dc in each st to end. Turn work.

Row 3 As row 2.

Row 4 1 ch to count as 1 dc. Work 1 dc in 3rd st from hook. ★ Miss 2 dc of 3rd row below, 1 tr in next 2 sts of 3rd row down placing hook into the single front loop of that st – miss the 2 dc on previous row, 1 dc in next 2 sts. ★ Repeat from ★ to ★ to end. Turn work.

Row 5 As row 2.

Row 6 1 ch to count as 1 dc. Miss 1st st of 3rd row below, 1 tr in next stitch of that row placing hook in front single loop. ★ 1 dc in next 2 sts of previous row, miss next 2 dc of 3rd row below, 1 tr in next 2 sts placing hook into single front loop – miss the 2 dc on previous row. ★ Repeat from ★ to ★ to end. Turn work.

Row 7 As row 2.

Rows 4, 5, 6 and 7 complete this pattern.

There is a definite right and wrong side to this fabric.

figure 86

figure 87

Step stitch   figure 87

Make a chain length – multiple of 8+2.

Row 1 3 ch to count as 1 tr. 1 tr in 5th ch from hook. 1 tr in each st to end. Turn work.

Row 2 3 ch to count as 1 tr. Miss 1st tr of previous row. ★ 1 tr in next 4 tr inserting hook from right to left under complete treble from *back* of work. 1 tr in next 4 tr inserting hook from right to left as before, from *front* of work. ★ Repeat from ★ to ★ to end. 1 tr in 3rd ch of turning chain. Turn work.

Row 3 3 ch to count as 1 tr. Miss 1st tr of previous row. 1 tr in next 2 tr inserting hook from back of work. ★ 1 tr in next 4 tr inserting hook from front of work. 1 tr in next 4 tr inserting hook from back of work. ★ Repeat from ★ to ★ to last 7 sts. 1 tr in next 4 tr inserting hook from front of work, 1 tr in next 2 tr inserting hook from back of work. 1 tr in 3rd turning chain. Turn work.

Row 4 3 ch to count as 1 tr. Miss 1st tr of previous row. ★ 1 tr in next 4 tr inserting hook from front of work. 1 tr in next 4 tr inserting hook from back of work. ★ Repeat from ★ to ★ to end. 1 tr in 3rd turning chain. Turn work.

Row 5 3 ch to count as 1 tr. Miss 1st tr of previous row. 1 tr in next 2 tr inserting hook from front of work. ★ 1 tr in next 4 tr inserting hook from back of work. 1 tr in next 4 tr inserting hook from front of work. ★ Repeat from ★ to ★ to last 7 sts. 1 tr in next 4 tr inserting hook from back of work, 1 tr in next 2 tr inserting hook from front of work. 1 tr in 3rd turning chain. Turn work.

Continue in this manner – giving a diagonal line by the placement of the treble stitch. This diagonal can be continued in the same direction or reversed – as in our sample.

This fabric is reversible.

43

Crossed double trebles

figure 88

Make a chain length – even number.

Row 1 1 ch to count as 1 dc. 1 dc in 3rd ch from hook. 1 dc in each ch to end. Turn work.

Row 2 4 ch to count as 1 d tr. 1 d tr in 7th st from hook. Placing hook behind the last d tr, 1 d tr in st before the stitch where the last d tr was worked. ★ Miss next st. 1 d tr in next st. 1 d tr in missed st placing hook behind last d tr worked. ★ Repeat from ★ to ★ to end. 1 d tr in 4th ch of turning chain. Turn work.

Row 3 1 ch to count as 1 dc. 1 dc in 3rd st from hook. 1 dc in each st to end. Turn work.

Rows 2 and 3 complete this pattern.

There is a definite right and wrong side to this fabric.

Surface zig–zag stitch

figure 89

Make a chain length – multiple of 4+2.

Row 1 3 ch to count as 1 tr. 1 tr in 6th ch from hook. 1 tr in next 2 ch. 1 tr into ch *before* first tr (figure 90). ★ Miss next ch. 1 tr in next 3 ch. 1 tr in ch missed. ★ Repeat from ★ to ★ to end. 1 tr in last chain. Turn work.

Row 2 3 ch to count as 1 tr. 1 tr in 6th st from hook. 1 tr in next 2 sts. 1 tr into st before first tr. ★ Miss next st, 1 tr in next 3 sts. 1 tr in stitch missed. ★ Repeat from ★ to ★ to end. 1 tr in 3rd ch of turning ch. Turn work.

Repeat row 1 throughout.

This is a reversible fabric.

Note: when working the treble into the stitch missed, the treble should be extended to the same length as the previous treble stitches.

figure 88

figure 89

figure 90

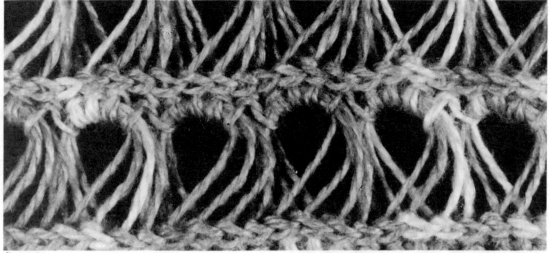

figure 91

Broom-handle stitch

figure 91

Make a chain length – multiple of 4+2.

Row 1 1 ch to count as 1 dc. 1 dc in 3rd ch from hook. 1 dc in each ch to end. Turn work.

Row 2 1 ch to count as 1 dc. Place a large wooden knitting needle or broom handle to act as a gauge behind work. Work in dc into each st placing yarn over the gauge (figure 92) to last st. Remove the gauge. 1 dc in turning ch. Turn work.

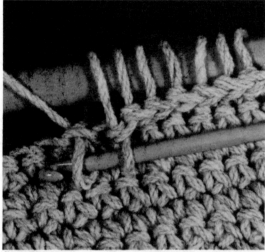

figure 92

Row 3 3 ch to count as 1 tr. ★ Place hook into 4 loops, work 4 dc into each group (figure 93). ★ Repeat from ★ to ★ to end. 1 tr in turning ch. Turn work.

Rows 2 and 3 complete this pattern.

There is a definite right and wrong side to this fabric.

figure 93

Star stitch figure 94

Make a chain length – multiple of 2.

Row 1 3 ch (yoh, insert hook into 2nd ch from hook, yoh and draw through yarn) twice. 5 loops on hook. Miss 1 ch. Insert hook into next ch and draw through yarn. Yoh and draw through all loops on hook. 1 ch.

★ (Yoh, insert hook into same ch as last st. Yoh and draw through yarn) twice. Miss 1 ch, insert hook into next ch and draw through yarn. Yoh and draw through all loops on hook. 1 ch. ★ Repeat from ★ to ★ to end. Turn work.

Row 2 1 ch (yoh, insert hook into 2nd ch from hook, yoh and draw through yarn) twice. Miss 1 st. Insert hook into next st and draw through yarn (6 loops on hook). Yoh and draw through all loops on hook (figure 95), 1 ch.

★ (Yoh, insert hook into same st as last st, yoh and draw through yarn) twice. Miss 1 st. Insert hook into next st and draw through yarn. Yoh and draw through all loops on hook. 1 ch. ★ Repeat from ★ to ★ to end. Turn work.

Row 2 is repeated throughout for this pattern.

This is a reversible fabric.

See the colour illustration (p49) which shows a tabard made in star stitch using Paton's Trident yarn in two colours for the main part of the outfit. The hem is trimmed with a *petal effect* using six toning colours. The same colours are used for tassels which form the fastening on the shoulders and the sides.

figure 94

figure 95

One-way star stitch

figure 96

Make a chain length – multiple of 2.

Row 1 1 ch. Insert hook into 2nd ch from hook. Yoh and draw through yarn, (insert hook into *next* ch, yoh and draw through yarn) 4 times. (6 loops on hook.) Yoh and draw through all loops on hook. 1 ch.

* Insert hook into hole at centre of last star. Yoh and draw through yarn. Insert hook into back loop of last st of same star. Yoh and draw through yarn. Insert hook into foundation ch where last loop of st was worked, yoh and draw through yarn. (Insert hook in next ch and draw through yarn) twice. (6 loops on hook.) Yoh and draw through all loops on hook. 1 ch. * Repeat from * to * to end. 1 tr into last ch. Break off yarn. Secure end and *do not turn work.*

Row 2 Sl st into 2nd st before centre star of previous row. 3 ch.

Insert hook into 2nd ch from hook and draw through yarn. Insert hook into next ch, yoh and draw through yarn. Insert hook into st before centre of star of last row, yoh and draw through yarn. Insert hook in centre hole of same star, yoh and draw through yarn. Insert hook into next st before the centre of next star, yoh and draw through yarn. (6 loops on hook.) Yoh and draw through all loops on hook. 1 ch.

* Insert hook into centre hole of star just formed, yoh and draw through yarn. Insert hook into back loop of last stitch of same star, yoh and draw through yarn. Insert hook into stitch before centre hole of next star in previous row, yoh and draw through yarn. Insert hook into centre hole of star in previous row, yoh and draw through yarn.

Insert hook into back loop of st before the centre hole of next star of previous row, yoh and draw through yarn. (6 loops on hook.) (figure 97). Yoh and draw through all loops on hook. 1 ch. * Repeat from * to * to end.

The last hook insertion is placed into the tr at the end of the last row. 1 tr into same position. Break off yarn. Secure end and *do not turn work.*

Repeat row 2 throughout.

There is a definite right and wrong side to this fabric.

figure 96

figure 97

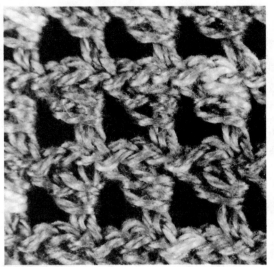

figure 98

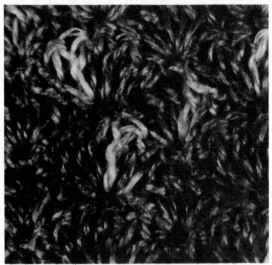

figure 99

Horizontal trebles

figure 98

Make a chain length – multiple of 3+1.

Row 1 1 ch to count as 1 dc. 1 dc in 3rd ch from hook. 1 dc in each ch to end. Turn work.

Row 2 3 ch to count as 1 tr. Working over ch just worked, work 1 h tr and 1 tr. ★ Miss 2 dc. 1 tr into next dc. Working over tr just worked, work 1 h tr and 1 tr. ★ Repeat from ★ to ★ to end. 1 tr in last ch. Turn work.

Row 3 1 ch. 1 sl st into 2nd ch from hook. 1 sl st into each st to end. Turn work.

Row 4 3 ch to count as 1 tr. Working over ch just worked, work 1 h tr and 1 tr. ★ Miss 2 sts. 1 tr into next sl st. Working over tr just worked, work 1 h tr and 1 tr. ★ Repeat from ★ to ★ to end. 1 tr in last sl st. Turn work.

Repeat rows 3 and 4 throughout.

There is a definite right and wrong side to this fabric. Either side will look pleasing.

Shell stitch   figure 99

Make a chain length – multiple of 8+3.

Row 1 Into 7th ch from hook work 5 tr. ★ Miss 3 ch. 1 dc in next ch. Miss 3 ch. 5 tr into next ch. ★ Repeat from ★ to ★ to end. Miss 3 ch. 1 dc in last ch. Turn work.

Row 2 3 ch to count as 1 tr. 2 tr into dc at base of ch. ★ 1 dc into centre tr of next 5 tr group. 5 tr into next dc. ★ Repeat from ★ to ★ to end. 3 tr in last ch of turning ch. Turn work.

Row 3 1 ch to count as 1 dc. ★ 5 tr into next dc, 1 dc into centre tr of next 5 tr group. ★ Repeat from ★ to ★ to end. 1 dc into 3rd ch of turning ch of last row. Turn work.

Rows 2 and 3 are repeated throughout for this pattern.

The fabric is reversible.

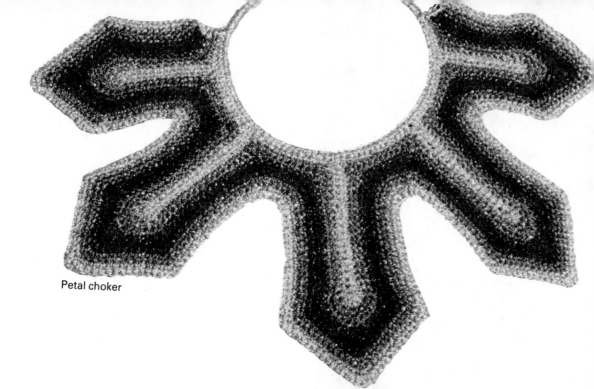

Petal choker

Tabard in star stitch

Leg warmers and pocket scarf

Hat in trebles in relief,
and scarf in treble stitch,
both trimmed with accordion stitch

below left Grey coat and scarf

below right Hand-spun wool from a Jacob's fleece was used
for this shawl made by Jean Leigh

Skirts, and waistcoat
with multiple loop stitch
decoration

Long skirt in squares

Belt using mohair covered rings

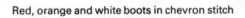

Red, orange and white boots in chevron stitch

Bullion stitch figure 100

Make a chain length.

Row 1 1 ch to count as 1 dc. 1 dc into 3rd ch from hook. 1 dc in each ch to end. Turn work.

Row 2 3 ch to count as 1 tr. Yoh 5 times (figure 101). Insert hook into 5th st from hook, yoh and draw through yarn and draw through all loops on hook. ★ Yoh 5 times. Insert hook into next st, yoh and draw through yarn and through all loops on hook. ★ Repeat from ★ to ★ to last st. 1 tr in last st. Turn work.

Row 3 1ch to count as 1 dc. 1 dc into 3rd st from hook. 1 dc in each st to end. Turn work.

Repeat rows 2 and 3 throughout for this pattern.

There is a definite right and wrong side to this fabric.

Note: This stitch requires practice before a good result is achieved.

figure 101

figure 100

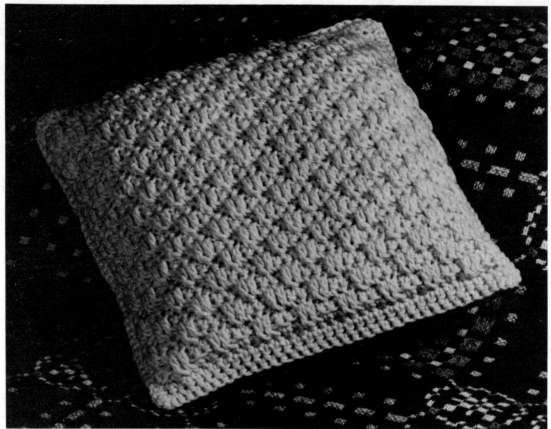

figure 102

Cushion in check stitch

figure 102

2×50gm balls of Patons Aran yarn and a number
5·50 ISR crochet hook should be used. The
cushion measures 12in (30·5cm) square.

Tension 6 sts, 5 rows to a 2in (5cm) square.

Work over 36 sts. When the two sides are
complete, sew together three sides, insert a
cushion pad slightly larger than the crochet
square, sew up fourth side. Alternatively, the dc
crochet method can be used to join the sides
(chapter 10).

All the stitches illustrated in this chapter could be
used for a cushion of this type.

The bags illustrated in the previous chapters
could also be made up using these stitches.

6 Open stitches

Open crochet stitches lend themselves easily to lacy designs. These stitches are quick to work and will be suitable for shawls, stoles, hats and head scarves. The mohair, lurex and pure wool fancy yarns are especially suitable for these articles. When using the more unusual yarns, such as string and parcel twines, beach bags and room dividers make good articles to work.

Five stitches are illustrated in this chapter and these should be practised using Double Knitting yarn and a number 4·50 ISR crochet hook.

Chain lace figure 103

Make a chain length – multiple of 5 + 1.

Row 1 8 ch. 1 dc into the 14th ch from hook. ★ 8 ch. Miss 4 ch. 1 dc into next chain. ★ Repeat from ★ to ★ to end. Turn work.

Row 2 14 ch. 1 dc into the 1st space, ★ 8 ch. 1 dc into the next space. ★ Repeat from ★ to ★ to end. Turn work.

Repeat row 2 throughout.

Note: This stitch can also be worked in circles, by working a chain length foundation and joining with a sl st.

figure 103

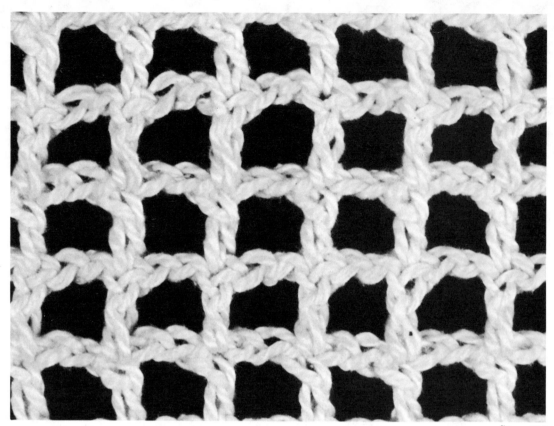

figure 104

Spaced trebles figure 104

Make a chain length – multiple of 3+1.

Row 1 5 ch to count as 1 tr, and 2 ch for space. 1 tr into 9th ch from hook. ★ 2 ch, miss 2 ch. 1 tr into next ch. ★ Repeat from ★ to ★ to end. Turn work.

Row 2 5 ch to count as 1 tr, and 2 ch for space. Miss 1st space. ★ 1 tr into next tr. 2 ch. Miss 2 ch. ★ Repeat from ★ to ★ to end. 1 tr into 4th ch of turning ch. Turn work.

Repeat row 2 throughout.

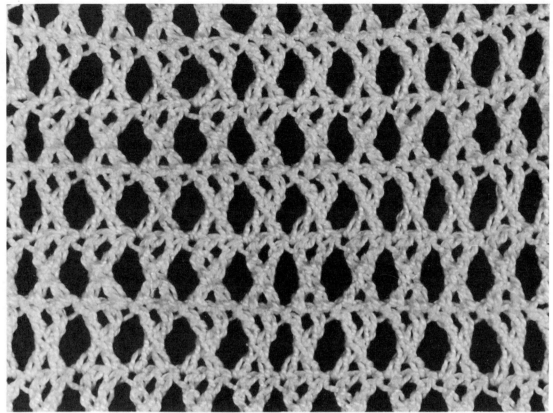

Crossed trebles figure 105

Make a chain length – multiple of 3.

Row 1 7 ch. Yoh, insert hook into the 5th ch from hook, yoh and draw through loop. Miss 4 ch, yoh, insert hook into next ch. Yoh and draw through loop (5 loops on hook). (Yoh and draw through 2 loops) 4 times. ★ Yoh twice, insert hook into next ch. Yoh and draw through loop. Yoh and draw through 2 loops, miss 1 ch, yoh, insert hook into next ch. Yoh and draw through loop (5 loops on hook). (Yoh and draw through 2 loops) 4 times. 1 ch. 1 tr into middle of cross. ★ Repeat from ★ to ★ to end. Turn work.

Row 2 7 ch. Yoh, insert hook into 5th st from hook, yoh and draw through loop, miss 4 sts. Yoh, insert hook into next st. Yoh and draw through loop (5 loops on hook). (Yoh and draw through 2 loops) 4 times. ★ Yoh twice, insert hook into next tr, yoh and draw through loop, yoh and draw through 2 loops, miss 1 ch. Yoh, insert hook into next tr, yoh and draw through loop, (yoh – figure 106 – and draw through 2 loops) 4 times. 1 ch. 1 tr into middle of cross. ★ Repeat from ★ to ★ to end. Turn work.

Repeat row 2 throughout.

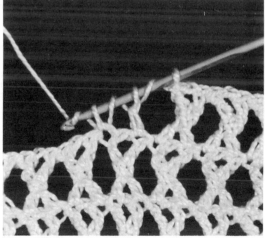

figure 106

Trebles and looped chain – striped fabric

figure 107

Make a foundation chain length – multiple of 19+7.

Row 1 3 ch to count as 1 tr. 1 tr into 5th ch from hook. 1 tr into next 5 ch. ★ 12 ch. Miss 12 ch. 1 tr into next 7 ch. ★ Repeat from ★ to ★ to end. Turn work.

Row 2 3 ch to count as 1 tr. 1 tr into 5th st from hook. 1 tr into next 5 tr. ★ 12 ch. Miss 12 ch. 1 tr into next 7 tr. ★ Repeat from ★ to ★ to end. Turn work.

Rows 3 and 4 Repeat row 2.

Row 5 3 ch to count as 1 tr. 1 tr into 5th st from hook. 1 tr into next 5 tr. ★ 6 ch. 1 dc over the 5 ch lengths below (figures 108 and 109). 6 ch. 1 tr into next 7 tr. ★ Repeat from ★ to ★ to end. Turn work.

For further repeats, work row 2 five times, and row 5 once.

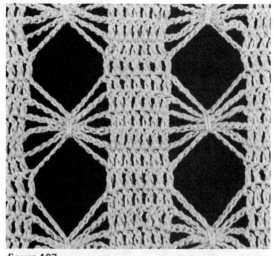

figure 107

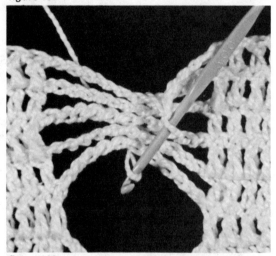

figure 108

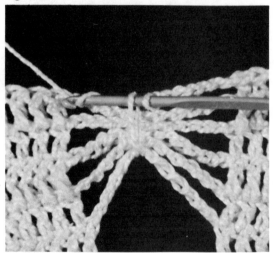

figure 109

Solomon's knot stitch

figure 110

This stitch is worked by extending the stitch on your hook – usually worked in groups of two, and so placed together to form a squared mesh.

To work Solomon's knot stitch Place a slip loop on your hook and extend the stitch to measure 1¼in (3cm). Yoh and hold this yarn between the thumb and the first finger of the left hand, drawing the yarn through the extended stitch on hook. Insert hook under the held yarn (figure 111) yoh and draw through loop. Yoh and draw through·both loops on hook. You have now worked one Solomon's knot stitch.

When working a fabric in this stitch, work a length of Solomon's knots as a foundation.

To work the second row sl st into 5th knot from hook. ★ 2 Solomon's knots. Sl st into 2nd knot on foundation. ★ Repeat from ★ to ★ to end. Turn work.

Repeat this second row throughout.

figure 110

figure 111

figure 112

Beach bag with round handles figure 112

Crossed trebles are used for the beach bag made with one ball of parcel twine and two hand–cut circular perspex handles. Number 5·50 ISR crochet hook is recommended for this twine. A length of fabric is worked over 45 chain stitches, working to the instructions for crossed trebles, for a length of 28in (71cm). The fabric should be folded in half, and sewn together at each side for a depth of 11in (28cm). A length of chain stitch is used to loop the top edge onto the circular handles for both sides.

Beach bag with oblong handles figure 112

Spaced trebles are used for the beach bag made with parcel twine and two hand–cut wooden handles. Number 5·50 ISR crochet hook is recommended for this twine. A length of fabric is worked over 40 chain stitches, working to the instructions for spaced trebles. Complete the bag as above.

Vegetable bag figure 113

One ball of fine parcel string worked in the chain lace forms this bag. Number 4·00 ISR crochet hook is recommended.

Tension approximately 8 ch to 2in (5cm).

Round 1 Fasten the string on to a 2in (5cm) diameter curtain ring and work 22 8 ch lengths, joining each length into the ring with a double crochet stitch (figure 114).

Round 2 Slip stitch along 4 ch of the first ch length loop, and continue in chain lace working 1 dc into each chain length. Continue in chain lace, working in rounds until the required bag depth is completed. Two double chain cords form the fastening. These should be threaded through each loop of the final round of chain lace.

figure 113

figure 114

Scarf/stole figure 115

Total length of scarf is 60in (152cm) excluding the fringe. 5 balls of Paton's 4–ply yarn and a number 4·00 ISR crochet hook are used for this scarf.

Tension approximately one Solomon's knot stitch to 1in (2·5cm).

The stole is worked in Solomon's knot stitch throughout, working over a foundation of 36 knot stitches. One further ball of yarn will be required if the fringe is worked. To work the fringe, place 6 lengths of yarn 12½in (32cm) long through each point at the end of the stole (see working methods, chapter 11, for full details of making fringes).

Hat figure 116

To work the hat (This hat will fit an average head size of 21/22in.) 1 ball of Twilley's Stalite yarn. Number 3·50 ISR crochet hook.

Tension 6 chain stitches=1¼in (3cm), for the lace; and 4½ stitches, 4 rows=1in (2·5cm) in the double dc stitch forming the band.

Make a chain length of 95 sts. Slip stitch into the first chain to make a circle.

Note: care should be taken not to twist the chain stitches.

Round 1 1 ch to count as 1 dc. Mark this ch st with a safety pin. Work 1 dc into the 3rd ch from hook. 1 dc into each ch to end of round. Sl st into the ch marked with a safety pin.

A second row of double crochet is then worked *into the same chain stitches* as the last row to give a very firm stitch. This completes the first round.

Round 2 1 ch to count as 1 dc. Remove safety pin from previous round, and mark this ch st. Work 1 dc into the 3rd st from hook. 1 dc into each st to end of round. Sl st into the ch st marked with the safety pin.

figure 115

A second row of dc is then worked *into the same stitch as* the last row to give a very firm stitch. This completes the second round.

Repeat round 2 three more times.

Round 6 ★ 6 ch. Miss 4 sts, 1 dc into the next st. ★ Repeat from ★ to ★ to end of round.

Round 7 Sl st into 3 ch of first loop. ★ 6 ch. 1 dc into next loop. ★ Repeat from ★ to ★ to end of round.

Repeat round 7 six more times.

To complete the hat, thread a 6in (15cm) length of yarn through each loop of the final round, draw up tightly and secure very firmly. Secure the cut ends.

figure 116

7 Textured effects

Once the basic stitches of the preceding chapters are mastered, interesting textures can be achieved. The textured effects in this chapter are worked in one colour of yarn to give the full impact of texture. Various colours have been introduced for further effect. All stitches should be worked on a sample piece before starting any of the suggested articles illustrated at the end of this chapter.

Loop stitch

used in the textured cushion – figure 117

There is a definite right and wrong side to this fabric.

Work to the required position for the loop stitch row.

Row 1 Wrong side of work facing.

1 ch to count as 1 dc. Begin loop st in 3rd st from hook. ★ Insert hook into next st and catch the yarn behind the second finger and draw through yarn leaving a loop over the first finger.

figure 117

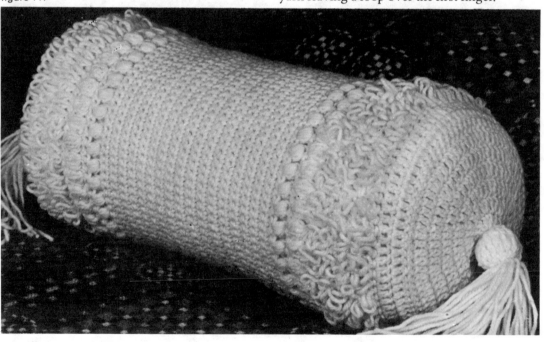

1²⁄₃in (4cm) long (figure 118). Slip finger out of loop, yoh (figure 119) and draw through both loops on hook. ★ Repeat from ★ to ★ to last st. 1 dc in turning chain of last row. Turn work.

Row 2 Right side of work facing.

1 ch to count as 1 dc. Begin loop st in 3rd st from hook. ★ Insert hook in *front* loop of next st. Yoh and draw through loop 1²⁄₃in (4cm) long. Remove hook. Insert hook into *both* loops of same st. Yoh and draw through loop, yoh and draw through both loops on hook. ★ Repeat from ★ to ★ to last st. 1 dc in turning chain of last row. Turn work.

Rows 1 and 2 are repeated for the required amount.

figure 118

Cluster or pine stitch

used in the textured cushion – figure 117

This stitch is usually worked with the right side facing. Work to the required position for the cluster stitch row.

Row 1 4 ch to count as 1 tr and 1 ch for space. Work first cluster in 7th st from hook. ★ (Yoh and insert hook into next st. Yoh and draw through yarn and extend to the length of a treble st) 5 times. Yoh (figure 120) and draw through all loops on hook. 1 ch. Miss next st. ★ Repeat from ★ to ★ to last st. 1 tr in turning chain. Turn work.

This completes the cluster stitch row. A row of trebles or dc is worked after this row placing the hook into each st of the last row.

figure 119

figure 120

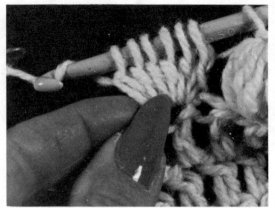

figure 121

Bobble stitch

used in the textured cushion – figure 117

This stitch is usually worked with the right side facing.

Work to the required position for the bobble stitch row.

Row 1 4 ch to count as 1 tr and 1 ch for space. Work 1st bobble in 7th st from hook. ★ (Yoh and insert hook into next st. Yoh and draw through yarn, yoh and draw through 2 loops) 6 times. Yoh (figure 121) and draw through all 7 loops on hook. 1 ch. Miss 1 st. ★ Repeat from ★ to ★ to last st. 1 tr in turning chain. Turn work.

This completes the bobble st. A row of trebles or dc is worked after this row, placing the hook into each st of the last row.

figure 123

figure 122

Chain fur stitch

used in the textured cushion – figure 122

This stitch is usually worked with the wrong side facing.

Work to the required position for the chain fur stitch row.

Row 1 10 ch. 1 dc into the 11th st from hook, placing the hook into the *back* loop of the st. ★ 10 ch. 1 dc into *back* loop of next st ★ (figure 123). Repeat from ★ to ★ to last st. 1 dc in turning ch. Turn work.

This completes the chain fur st. A row of trebles or dc is worked after this row, placing hook into the back loop of each st of the last row.

Cut fur stitch figure 124

A crochet mesh is the basis for this fabric. Into this mesh place 2 cut lengths of yarn 2½ in (6cm) long, as shown in figure 125.

The mesh is worked over an uneven chain length.

Row 1 1 dc into 3rd ch from hook. ★ 1 ch, miss 1 ch to form a space. 1 dc into next ch. ★ Repeat from ★ to ★ to end. Turn work.

Row 2 1 ch to count as 1 dc. 1 dc into first 1 ch space. ★ 1 ch, 1 dc into next 1 ch space. ★ Repeat from ★ to ★ to end. 1 ch. 1 dc in turning chain. Turn work.

Repeat rows 1 and 2 for the required amount.

figure 124

Popcorn stitch

used in the textured cushion – figure 122

This stitch is usually worked with the right side facing.

Work to the required position for the popcorn stitch row.

Row 1 3 ch to count as 1 tr. 5 tr into 5th st from hook. Remove hook leaving the working st free. Insert hook into the 5th st back from free st. Catch the working st and draw through this position (figure 126). ★ 1 ch, miss 1 st. 5 tr in next st. Remove hook leaving working st free. Insert hook into the 5th st back from free st. Catch working st and draw through this position. ★ Repeat from ★ to ★ to last st. 1 tr in turning chain. Turn work.

This completes the popcorn stitch row. A row of tr or dc is worked after this row, placing the hook into each st of the last row.

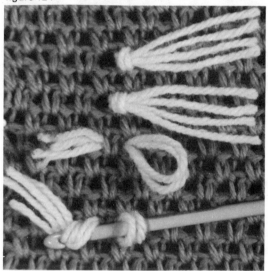

figure 125

figure 126

Block stitch

used in the textured cushion – figure 122

This stitch is usually worked with the right side facing.

Work to the required position for the block stitch row.

Row 1 3 ch to count as 1 tr for the *block*. (Yoh (figure 127), place hook in front of chain length and place yoh, figure 128) 3 times (7 loops on hook). Insert hook into 5th st from hook. Yoh and draw through all loops on hook extending the st to the treble length. ★ 1 ch, miss 1 st. 1 tr in next st. (Yoh, place hook in front of tr and free yarn of last st, yoh) 3 times (7 loops on hook). Insert hook into next st, yoh (figure 129) and draw through all loops on hook extending st to treble length. ★ Repeat from ★ to ★ to end.

Note: there will be one free yarn length behind the last block made. This completes the block stitch row.

A row of tr or dc is worked after this row, placing the hook into each stitch of the last row.

Textured cushions

figures 117 and 122

Each cushion requires 8×50gm balls of Paton's Capstan yarn. Number 5·50 ISR crochet hook.

Tension 6 dc and 9 rows=2in (5cm).

Measurements circumference 24in (61cm); length 16in (40cm); diameter 7½in (19cm).

Both cushions are worked over 72 stitches, working in rows as follows:

figure 127

figure 128

figure 129

Grey jumper in double crochet, with red, white and black stripes

Grey jumper with surface stitching

Black shawl with flower motif

Detail of flower motif

Patchwork jacket using triangles

Blue and white jacket in zig-zag stitch

Red bolero using circles

Gold clutch bag using woven ribbon

Cushion 1 figure 117

2 rows treble
6 rows loop stitch
1 row dc
1 row bobble stitch
1 row dc
1 row cluster stitch ★★
35 rows dc
Work from ★★ in reverse order to complete cushion.

To make up the cushion Sew together the long edges. Make two crochet circles working in treble stitch (chapter 10) – six rounds. Sew one circle to one end, insert cushion pad made slightly larger than the measurements of the crochet, sew second circle on remaining end. Decorative tassels can be sewn on to the centres of each circle (see chapter 11 for working methods).

Cushion 2 figure 122

2 rows tr
1 row chain fur stitch
1 row tr
1 row chain fur stitch
1 row tr
1 row chain fur stitch
2 rows dc
1 row block stitch
2 rows dc
1 row popcorn stitch
2 rows dc
1 row block stitch ★★
27 rows dc
Work from ★★ in reverse order to complete cushion.

To make up this cushion
Follow the instructions for the first cushion.

figure 130

Accordion stitch figure 130

This is an attractive stitch suitable for use as a decoration or edging stitch. The stitch can be worked in one colour or toning colours.

A crochet mesh has to be worked first as a base.

To work the crochet mesh Work a chain length – multiple of 2+1.

Row 1 4 ch to count as 1 tr and 1 ch space. 1 tr into 7th chain from hook. ★ 1 ch, miss 1 ch, 1 tr into next ch. ★ Repeat from ★ to ★ to end. Turn work.

Row 2 4 ch to count as one tr and 1 ch space. 1 tr into 7th st from hook. ★ 1 ch, miss 1 st. 1 tr into next st. ★ Repeat from ★ to ★ to end. End with 1 tr in 3rd ch of turning ch. Turn work.

Repeat row 2 for the required amount.

To work the accordion stitch Work from the right side of fabric. Make a slip loop and join yarn on to the starting position for the accordion stitch. Work 3 ch to count as first treble stitch. Work 3 trebles over each bar of mesh inserting the hook under the complete bar of the mesh, ie over a treble or the chain stitch between the trebles. Various lines and patterns can be achieved according to the direction of the trebles.

73

Usually, however, the accordion stitch is worked up a treble, along the chain running from the top of the stitch, down the next treble stitch, and along the next chain running from the base of the stitch.

Multiple loop stitch using a ruler figure 131

Work to the required position for the multiple loop stitch.

This stitch is worked with the wrong side of work facing.

Take a ruler 1¼in (3cm) wide and approximately the same length as the width of work. With a separate ball of yarn, wind the yarn round the ruler, 3 times for each stitch to be worked on your row. Begin the row with 1 ch. Place the ruler with the yarn behind your work, * insert hook into next st and through 3 loops on the ruler. Yoh and draw through these loops and through stitch of previous row (2 loops on hook), yoh and draw through both loops on hook. * Repeat from * to * to last st. 1 dc in turning chain. Turn work.

This completes the loop stitch row. One or more rows of dc should be worked before the next multiple loop stitch row is worked.

The same colour yarn can be used throughout or choose toning shades of one colour for added effect.

figure 131

Scarf

The colour illustration (p50) shows a scarf worked in treble stitch, and trimmed with accordion stitch decoration on both ends. 6×25gm balls of Paton's Trident DK yarn are required for the main part of the scarf and oddments of Trident yarn in 5 contrasting colours are used for the trim.

Tension 8 tr and 4 rows=2in (5cm). Number 4·50 ISR crochet hook is used.

Work over 31 sts as follows: 5 rows in mesh for accordion stitch trim (p73), 96 rows in treble stitch, followed by 5 more rows in mesh.

Work the accordion stitch trim to both ends.

Hat

The colour illustration (p50) shows a hat, worked in 'trebles in relief' and trimmed with accordion stitch decoration. 6×25gm balls of Paton's Trident DK yarn are required for the main part of the hat and oddments of Trident yarn in 5 contrasting colours are used for the trim.

Tension 8 sts and 4 rows=2in (5cm). Number 4·50 ISR crochet hook is used.

Work 50 rows over 32 stitches in *trebles in relief* (p37). Join together by sewing the foundation edge to the edge of the last row worked. The top of the hat is worked by running a double length of yarn through one open end, and gathering the work tightly together. Secure the ends very firmly. At the other end, work 5 rows over 88 stitches in mesh stitch to take the accordion trim, placing the hook into the last stitch at the edge of the crochet. Turn the mesh stitch crochet back over the treble in relief, and work the accordion stitch, so it is placed on the right side of the hat.

Three-quarter length coat

The colour illustration (p50) also shows a grey three-quarter length coat worked in treble stitch and trimmed with accordion stitch decoration round the edges. 29×25gm balls of Paton's Trident DK yarn are required for the main part of the coat, and 4×25gm balls each of Paton's Trident DK yarn in each of 5 contrasting colours are used for the trim.

Tension 8 tr and 4 rows=2in (5cm). Number 4·50 ISR crochet hook is used.

A calico toile was used to obtain this garment (for details see working methods, chapter 11).

Waistcoat

The colour illustration (p51) shows a waistcoat worked in treble stitch worked alternatively with double crochet and trimmed with the multiple loop stitch decoration. 4×25gm balls of Paton's Trident DK yarn are required for the main part of the waistcoat, and oddments of Trident yarn in each of 5 contrasting colours are used for the trim.

Tension 8 sts and 6 rows (3 tr and 3 dc)=2in (5cm). Number 4·50 ISR crochet hook is used.

A calico toile was used to obtain this garment (for details see working methods, chapter 11). A six-gored skirt is worn with the waistcoat. This was also made from a calico toile.

8 Crochet stitches using colour for effect

Several techniques which rely on the use of colour to give effect are explained in this chapter. The colours can be worked as an integral part of the crochet, or added after a base stitch has been worked. All the stitches form a fabric which could be used for most articles of clothing and accessories, etc. Always exercise care and thought when selecting your yarn colours and textures.

One colour or several different colours can be used for the *chevron stitch*, changing your yarn for different rows:

Chevron stitch in double crochet figure 132

Make a chain length – multiple of 16 + 3.

Row 1 1 ch, insert hook into 3rd ch from hook, yoh and draw through yarn, insert hook into next ch, yoh and draw through yarn, yoh and draw through all loops on hook. ★ 1 dc in next 6 ch. 3 dc into next ch. 1 dc in next 6 ch. (Insert hook into next ch, yoh and draw through loop) 3 times, yoh and draw through all 4 loops on hook, ie 2 dc decreased. ★ Repeat from ★ to ★ to end. Turn work.

Note: for all rows following, place the hook in the *back single* loop of each stitch. This gives the ridged effect.

Row 2 2 ch. Insert hook into 2nd st from hook, decrease 2 dc over next 3 sts. ★ 1 dc in next 6 dc. 3 dc into next ch. 1 dc in next 6 dc. Decrease 2 dc over next 3 sts. ★ Repeat from ★ to ★ to end. Turn work.

Row 2 is repeated throughout, changing colours as wanted.

figure 132

76

Chevron stitch in trebles

figure 133

Make a chain length – multiple of 17+2.

Row 1 3 ch to count as 1 tr. Work 3 tr into 5th ch from hook. ★ 1 tr into next 5 ch, decrease 1 tr (see page 31; chapter 3) 3 times over the next 6 sts. 1 tr into next 5 ch, 4 tr in next ch. ★ Repeat from ★ to ★ to end. Turn work.

Row 2 3 ch to count as 1 tr, 3 tr into 5th st from hook. ★ 1 tr into next 5 sts. Decrease 1 tr 3 times over next 6 sts. 1 tr into next 5 sts. 4 tr into next st. ★ Repeat from ★ to ★ to end. Turn work.

Row 2 is repeated throughout, changing colours as wanted.

figure 133

Zig-zag stitch figure 134

This stitch forms an attractive fabric. It is firm and warm – contrasting colours should be used to give the best effect. The stitch is basically dc throughout, working over various rows below the current row.

Work a chain length – multiple of 10+1.

Row 1 1 ch to count as 1 dc. 1 dc in 3rd ch from hook, 1 dc in each ch to end. Turn work.

Row 2 1 ch to count as 1 dc. 1 dc in 3rd st from hook. 1 dc in each st to end. Turn work.

Rows 3 to 6 Repeat row 2. Break off yarn.

Row 7 Introduce new colour. Zig-zag row.
1 ch to count as 1 dc.
★ 1 dc in next st, placing hook into 2nd row down.
1 dc in next st, placing hook into 3rd row down.
1 dc in next st, placing hook into 4th row down.
1 dc in next st, placing hook into 5th row down.
1 dc in next st, placing hook into 6th row down (figure 135).

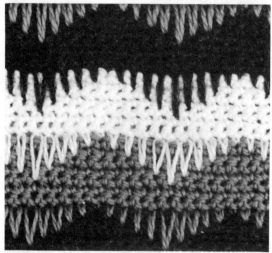

figure 134

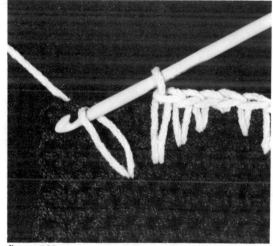

figure 135

1 dc in next st, placing hook into 5th row down.
1 dc in next st, placing hook into 4th row down.
1 dc in next st, placing hook into 3rd row down.
1 dc in next st, placing hook into 2nd row down.
1 dc in next st, placing hook into last row
worked. ★ Repeat from ★ to ★ to end of row,
ending with last dc in turning chain of last row.

Turn work.

Work 5 rows in dc before repeating the zig-zag
row and introducing the next colour.

Figures 136, 137 and 138 illustrate various effects
which can be obtained by altering the sequence
of hook insertions.

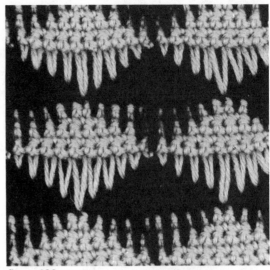

figure 136

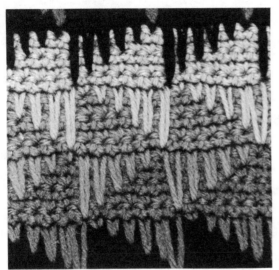

figure 137

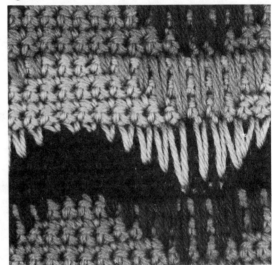

figure 138

Woven fabrics

Many experimental fabrics can be formed by using this technique. Basically a crochet mesh is worked in trebles as explained in chapter 7 for accordion braiding (p73). Using this mesh, various yarns and other materials such as ribbons and commercial braids can be threaded through the mesh (figure 139).

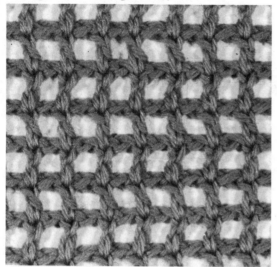

figure 139

figure 140

Figure 140 uses thin ribbon – the ribbon is threaded vertically, under one bar, and over two bars; each new row is started one bar down to give a diagonal appearance.

Figure 141 uses groups of yarn. One group of 4 threads is placed vertically, working over one bar, and under one bar of the crochet mesh. The second group of 4 threads is placed horizontally, working over one bar, and under one bar of the crochet mesh. The threads being woven into the mesh are usually of contrasting colours.

figure 141

Stitches using colour to form stripes

Colour can be introduced to plain crochet stitches by working in various colours to form stripes. Interest is added by varying the width of the stripes.

The colour illustration (p49) shows a pair of leg warmers using stripes as a feature.

The colour illustration (p69) also shows the use of stripes to give effect to a plain jumper.

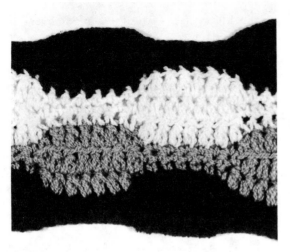

figure 142

Three-colour patterns

figure 142

Colours A, B and C.

With colour A make a chain length – multiple of 14+7.

Row 1 1 ch to count as 1 dc. 1 dc in 3rd ch from hook. 1 dc in next 5 ch. ★ 1 tr in next 7ch. 1 dc in next 7 ch. ★ Repeat from ★ to ★ to end. Turn work.

Row 2 1 ch to count as 1 dc. 1 dc in 3rd st from hook. 1 dc in next 5 ch. ★ 1 tr in next 7 sts. 1 dc in next 7 sts. ★ Repeat from ★ to ★ to end. Turn work.

Row 3 As row 2. Break off yarn and turn work.

Row 4 Join in colour B. 3 ch to count as 1 tr. 1 tr in 5th st from hook. 1 tr in next 5 sts. ★ 1 dc in next 7 sts. 1 tr in next 7 sts. ★ Repeat from ★ to ★ to end. Turn work.

Rows 5 and 6 As row 4. Break off yarn and turn work.

Join in colour C and repeat row 2, 3 times.

Continue changing colours in rotation every 3 rows, repeating row 4, 3 times, and row 2, 3 times.

80

figure 143

Two-colour fabric

figure 143

Colour A. Make a chain length – multiple of 6+1.

Row 1 3 ch to count as 1 tr. 1 tr in 5th chain from hook. 1 tr in next 2 ch. Miss 2 ch. 1 dc in next ch. ★ 3 ch. 1 tr in next 3 ch. Miss 2 ch. 1 dc in next ch. ★ Repeat from ★ to ★ to end. Break off yarn and secure. Turn work.

Row 2 Join in colour B by slip stitching on to the first chain length. 3 ch. 3 tr into same 3 ch length, ★ 1 dc into next 3 ch length. 3 ch. 3 tr into same 3 ch length. ★ Repeat from ★ to ★ to end. Break off yarn and secure. Turn work.

Repeat row 2 throughout, changing colours alternately.

Two-colour fabric with surface stitching figure 144

The main fabric is worked in treble stitch in one colour, over a chain length of a multiple of 6+1.

The second colour is introduced by working the surface stitch as follows: work from the right side of the fabric. Insert hook under the 1st treble on right-hand side of work and draw through a slip loop. Work 1 dc. 7 ch, insert hook under the 4th tr on the 3rd row above, work 1 dc. ★ 7 ch, miss 5 tr on 1st row, work 1 dc under the next tr, 7 ch, miss 5 tr on 3rd row above, work 1 dc under next tr. ★ Repeat from ★ to ★ to end.

When working the second zig-zag row let the dc meet on each point.

figure 144

Two-colour fabric

figure 145

Colour A. Make a chain length of uneven number.

Row 1 1 ch to count as 1 dc. 1 dc in 3rd ch from hook. 1 dc into each ch to end. Break off yarn. Turn work.

Row 2 Colour B. Join in new yarn and work 3 ch to count as 1 tr. Miss 1 dc. 1 d tr in chain below next dc. Work 1 tr into next dc. ★ Miss next dc and work 1 d tr into ch below next dc. 1 tr in next dc. ★ Repeat from ★ to ★ to end. Break off yarn and turn work.

Row 3 Colour A. Join in colour A and work 1 ch to count as 1 dc. 1 dc into 3rd st from hook. 1 dc into each st to end. Break off yarn and turn work.

Row 4 Colour B. Join in colour B and work 3 ch to count as 1 tr. Miss 1 dc. ★ 1 tr into next dc. Miss next dc. 1 d tr into tr below, passing hook

figure 145

from right to left under this stitch. ★ Repeat from ★ to ★ to end. Break off yarn and turn work.

Repeat rows 3 and 4 throughout.

House boots

The colour illustration (p52) shows house boots made in the chevron stitch using trebles and double crochet stitches.

A leather sole forms the base (chapter 12). These boots were worked from the top downwards, working in rounds and using a new colour for each round. From the heel onwards, double crochet and the same colour sequence completes the boot. Use Paton's DK yarn, 2×25gm balls in each of 5 toning colours. Hook size number 4·50 ISR.

Jacket

The colour illustration (p71) shows a jacket made in dark blue, light blue and white yarn by Patons. 5×50gm in dark blue, 4×50gm in light blue, 4×50gm in white. Hook size number 4·50 ISR. The zig-zag stitch (p77) is used, working the bands and cuffs in the dark blue yarn. A calico toile was used to make this garment.

Evening bag

The colour illustration (p72) shows an evening bag using the woven fabric technique. Twilley's Goldfinger yarn is recommended with a number 2·50 ISR hook. Make a straight piece of crochet to measure 9½in (24cm) by 15in (38cm). Ribbon and braid is then placed through the crochet. Sew together the two sides to give a bag depth of 5in (13cm). Vilene interlining and a satin lining may be placed inside.

Leg warmers

The colour illustration (p49) shows leg warmers made in Paton's Trident yarn using a cream base colour and four toning colours for the stripes. 4×25gm balls are required for the main colour, plus oddments for stripes. Hook size number 4·50 ISR.

Work in continuous rounds over a 48-length chain, working one round in treble stitch and one round in double crochet stitch. The leg warmers illustrated measure 19in (48cm). A cord and tassel decorate the top edge.

Jumper

The colour illustration (p69) shows a jumper made entirely in double crochet using Paton's Trident DK yarn. The main colour is light grey; red, white and black form the stripes. 19×25gm grey, 3×25gm in white, red and black. (Total of 28 balls.) Hook size number 4·50 ISR. A calico toile was used to make this garment.

Two belts

Figures 146(a) and (b) illustrate two belts using the woven fabric technique. Twilley's Lystwist yarn in black is used for the base mesh in example (a); Twilley's Cortina yarn in black is used for the base mesh in example (b); Twilley's Lystwist yarn is used for the weaving in (a); and a tubular cord is used in (b). Figure 147 shows the finished belt (b).

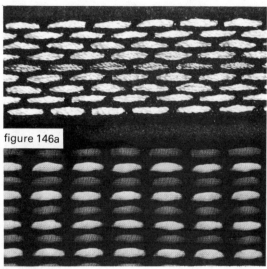

figure 146a

figure 146b

figure 147

9 Filet crochet

Filet crochet refers to a type of crochet lace; *filet* being the French for net. This work has an open, lacy appearance when worked in fine yarns.

Many tablecloths were trimmed with this type of work at the end of the nineteenth century using slightly thicker yarns and hooks, and examples are still to be found on Victorian tablecloths using this type of lace. The same technique can be used to make very attractive trimmings to white petticoats but nowadays thicker yarns and hook sizes are more popular.

Figure 148 illustrates crochet filet lace on a handkerchief.

There are two stitches used in filet crochet: the chain and the treble. First you should practise the open filet stitch.

figure 148

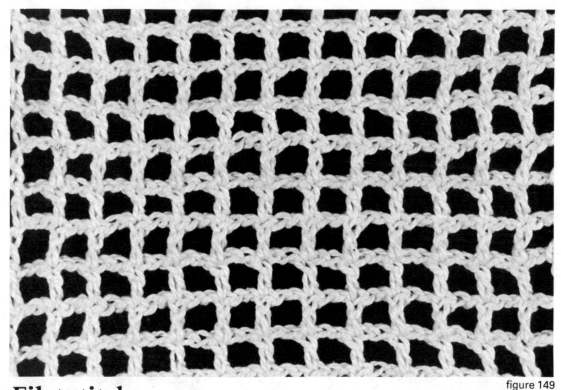
figure 149

Filet stitch   figure 149

Make a foundation chain – multiple of 3+1.

Row 1 5 ch to count as 1 tr and 2 ch for space. 1 tr
into 9th ch from hook, ★ 2 ch, miss 2 ch, 1 tr into
next ch. ★ Repeat from ★ to ★ to end. Turn work.

Row 2 5 ch to count as 1 tr and 2 ch for space.
Miss first space. ★ 1 tr into next tr, 2 ch, miss 2
ch. ★ Repeat from ★ to ★ to end. 1 tr into 4th ch of
turning chain. Turn work.

Repeat row 2 throughout.

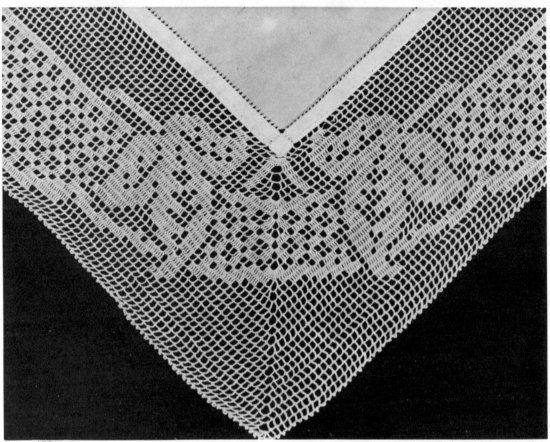

figure 150

Blocks and spaces

When the filet net is mastered you can incorporate patterns by working blocks of tr in place of a space. A block consists of 4 trs. A space consists of 1 tr, 2 ch, 1 tr. But remember: the tr of one block forms the tr of the next block or space, and vice versa.

To design your own patterns, use some squared paper. Let each square represent one space or one block for each row.

To form blocks in this mesh: work 1 tr into *each* ch of the space below.

To work a space over a block: work 1 ch over *each* tr of the block below.

Figure 150 illustrates in detail the filet lace handkerchief made by the late Mrs Sarah Pethes when she was a schoolgirl in Brasso, Transylvania (Romania) about sixty years ago. The lace measures 2¾in (7cm) and consists of 30 rows, which reveals the fineness of the work.

Large filet mesh stitch

figure 151

A larger filet mesh can be worked using double trebles – this makes an attractive fabric for stoles and shawls and is very quick to work. It also makes a good background for surface stitch embroidery and woven yarns.

Make a foundation chain – multiple of 4+1.

Row 1 7 ch to count as 1 d tr and 3 ch for space, 1 d tr into 12th ch from hook. ★ 3 ch, miss 3 ch. 1 d tr into next ch. ★ Repeat from ★ to ★ to end. Turn work.

Row 2 7 ch to count as 1 d tr and 3 ch for space, miss first space. ★ 1 d tr into next d tr, 3 ch, miss 3 ch. ★ Repeat from ★ to ★ to end. 1 d tr into 4th ch of turning chain. Turn work.

Repeat row 2 throughout.

To form blocks in this mesh, work 1 d tr into each ch of the space below.

To work a space over a block, work 1 ch over each d tr of the block below.

Chart designing

Figure 152 illustrates a charted design with the rows numbered. Instructions are given in detail to work this design. Practise this example before starting your own designs.

Figure 153 illustrates the crochet worked from this chart.

Make a chain length – 22 ch.

Row 1 5 ch to count as 1 tr and 2 ch for space. 1 tr into 9th ch from hook. ★ 2 ch, miss 2 ch, 1 tr into next ch. ★ Repeat from ★ to ★ to end. Turn work.

Row 2 5 ch to count as 1 tr and 2 ch for space. Miss first 2 ch space. 1 tr into next tr. (1 tr into next 2 ch, 1 tr in next tr) twice. 2 ch, miss 2 ch, 1 tr in next tr. (1 tr into next 2 ch, 1 tr in next tr) twice. 2 ch. 1 tr into 3rd ch of turning chain. Turn work.

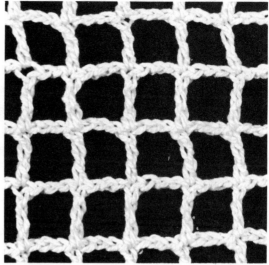

figure 151

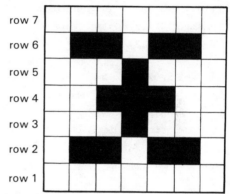

row 7
row 6
row 5
row 4
row 3
row 2
row 1

figure 152

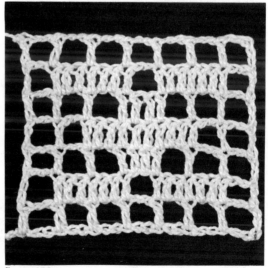

figure 153

Row 3 5 ch to count as 1 tr and 2 ch for space. Miss first 2 ch space, 1 tr into next tr. (2 ch, miss 2 tr, 1 tr into next tr) twice. 1 tr in next 2 ch, 1 tr in next tr. (2 ch, miss 2 tr, 1 tr into next tr) twice. 2 ch, miss 2 ch. 1 tr into 3rd ch of turning chain. Turn work.

Row 4 5 ch to count as 1 tr and 2 ch for space. Miss first 2 ch space. 1 tr into next tr. 2 ch, miss 2 ch. 1 tr into next tr. 1 tr in next 2 ch. 1 tr in next 4 tr. 1 tr in next 2 ch. 1 tr in next tr. 2 ch, miss 2 ch. 1 tr in next tr. 2 ch, miss 2 ch. 1 tr in 3rd ch of turning chain. Turn work.

Row 5 5 ch to count as 1 tr and 2 ch for space. Miss first 2 ch space. 1 tr into next tr. (2 ch, miss 2 sts. 1 tr into next tr) twice. 1 tr into next 3 tr. (2 ch, miss 2 sts. 1 tr into next tr) twice. 2 ch. 1 tr into 3rd ch of turning chain. Turn work.

Row 6 5 ch to count as 1 tr and 2 ch for space. Miss first 2 ch space. 1 tr into next tr. (1 tr into next 2 ch. 1 tr into next tr) twice. 2 ch, miss 2 tr. 1 tr into next tr. (1 tr into next 2 ch. 1 tr into next tr) twice. 2 ch, miss 2 ch. 1 tr into 3rd chain of turning chain. Turn work.

Row 7 5 ch to count as 1 tr and 2 ch for space. Miss first 2 ch space. 1 tr into next tr ★ 2 ch, miss 2 sts. 1 tr into next st. ★ Repeat from ★ to ★ to end. Last tr is worked into 3rd ch of turning chain. End work.

Shawl

The colour illustration (p70) shows a black shawl made entirely in the large filet mesh stitch. Surface embroidery has been used to decorate the centre of the shawl – alternatively the *block* technique could be used, working double trebles over four squares, and two squares, (respectively) to give a large blocked square or a smaller blocked square.

To work the shawl you will need 12×25gm balls of Twilley's Cortina yarn. Number 3·00 ISR crochet hook. Oddments of contrasting yarns will be required for the embroidery.

Tension 5 ch spaces and 6 rows=3in (7·5cm) square. Measurements of the shawl are approximately 52in (132cm) by 34in (86·5cm) excluding the fringe.

Work a chain length of 320 ch.

Follow the instructions for the large filet mesh stitch (page 87).

To shape the edge of the shawl: decrease one space by omitting the 3 ch worked between two d tr on the second space in from the edge on both sides.

Shape the sides of the shawl on the 5th row, and every alternate row until 46 spaces remain.

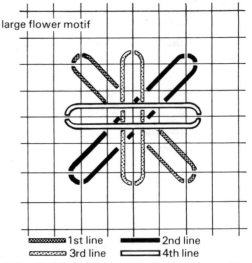

large flower motif

| ▩▩▩ 1st line | ▬▬ 2nd line |
| ▭▭ 3rd line | ▭▭ 4th line |

Note: the grid lines represent the lines formed by the crochet stitches

figure 154a

Then work one decreased space on both sides on every row until 2 spaces remain. End work.

A fringe improves the sides – 10 lengths of yarn 14in (36cm) long are looped through each space on the shaped edges (see chapter 11 for details of attaching the fringe).

The embroidered motifs (colour illustration p70) can be added to the large filet mesh to form a border or an all-over design. Figure 154(a) illustrates the working of the motif. Take double thicknesses of a contrasting yarn and work over the crochet mesh following the first line, then the second line, followed by the third line and the fourth line. Work each step three times. Complete motif by weaving a line over and under the centre of each group. Fasten all ends securely and neatly.

For the small motif, follow figure 154(b) using the same technique.

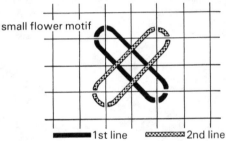

small flower motif

━━━ 1st line   ∞∞∞∞ 2nd line

Note: the grid lines represent the lines formed by the crochet stitches

figure 154b

Scarf

Figure 155 illustrates a long tie scarf made in Twilley's Lystwist yarn. Two balls are required and a number 2·50 ISR crochet hook.

Tension 5 space=3in (7·5cm) approximately.

Make a chain length – 73 ch.

Follow the instructions for the large filet mesh stitch, working a border to each end of the scarf by working one row in spaces, and one row completely in blocks. Five block rows complete the border. A 9in (23cm) fringe finishes the edge. The total length of this scarf is approximately 56in (142cm) long, excluding the fringe.

figure 155

10 Fabrics

This chapter covers methods of making interesting fabrics other than the conventional patterns already mentioned, eg circles, squares and various types of patchwork.

Various techniques are explained in detail and suggestions for articles to make are illustrated at the end of the chapter, and the working methods for using these fabrics are explained in the following chapter.

Circles and squares

Circles and squares can be made totally in one colour, or in various colours and textures. However, you should master how to make a simple flat circle first – using one colour.

To work a circle

illustrated in figure 157

Make a chain length – 5 ch. Join with a slip stitch to form a circle.

Round 1 3 ch to count as 1 tr. 11 tr into the circle. Join with a sl st into the 3rd ch at start of round.

Round 2 3 ch to count as 1 tr (figure 156). 2 tr into each tr of first round. 1 tr into base of 3 ch (ie 12 pairs of tr have been worked). Sl st into 3rd ch at start of round.

figure 156

Round 3 3 ch to count as 1 tr. 1 tr into next tr. ★ 2 tr into next tr. 1 tr into next tr. ★ Repeat from ★ to ★ to end. 1 tr into base stitch of 3 ch at start of round. Sl st into 3rd ch.

figure 157

Round 4 and all following rounds Continue in this manner, increasing by one the number of single trebles between each increase on each new round. See figure 157 showing several completed rounds.

To work a square

illustrated in the evening bag – figure 158

5 colours are used for this square – A, B, C, D, and E.

Colour A. Work 8 chain. Join with a slip stitch to form a circle.

Round 1 1 ch to count as 1 dc. 15 dc into the circle. Sl st to ch at start of round. Break off colour A. Join in colour B.

Round 2 (7 ch. Miss 3 dc. Sl st into next dc) four times.

Round 3 Sl st over 2 ch. Into 1st space work 3 ch to count as 1 tr. 3 tr into *same* space, 5 ch. 4 tr into *same* space. (Work 4 tr, 5 ch and 4 tr into next space) 3 times. Sl st into 3rd ch at start of round. Break off colour B. Join in colour C into 3rd ch of a 5 ch space.

Round 4 1 ch to count as 1 dc. ★ 10 ch. Miss 4 tr, 1 dc into space between tr, 10 ch. Miss 4 tr. 1 dc into next 5 ch space. ★ Repeat from ★ to ★ 3 times more, ending with a sl st into the 1st ch at start of round in place of 1 dc.

Round 5 Sl st over 2 ch. Work 3 ch to count as 1 tr, 7 tr into 1st space. 8 tr into next 10 ch space. 5 ch. ★ (8 tr into next 10 ch space) twice, 5 ch. ★ Repeat from ★ to ★ to end of round. Sl st into 3rd ch at start of round. Break off yarn and join in colour D to right side edge of a 5 ch space.

Round 6 1 ch to count as 1 dc. Into same space work 1 h tr, 1 tr, 3 ch, 1 tr, 1 h tr, 1 dc. 1 dc into next 16 sts. (Into next 5 ch space work 1 dc, 1 h tr, 1 tr, 3 ch, 1 tr, 1 h tr, 1 dc followed by 1 dc into the next 16 sts) 3 times. Sl st into chain at the start of the round. Break off yarn and join in colour E.

Round 7 Into each stitch work 1 dc. Work 3 dc into 1 stitch at the corners. End work.

figure 158

Evening bag figure 158

1 ball of Twilley's Lyscordet yarn is used for the main colour – colour E; 4 contrasting balls of Twilley's Goldfinger yarn or Lystwist yarn for colours A, B, C and D. Number 2·50 ISR crochet hook.

Tension one square measures approximately 4in (10cm).

To work the base of the bag
Work a flat circle as explained at the start of this chapter in colour E working six rounds 5½in(14cm). Continue *without* increasing as follows:

Round 7 3 ch to count as 1 tr. ★ 1 ch, miss 1 st, 1 tr in next st. ★ Repeat from ★ to ★ to end of round. 1 ch, miss 1 st, sl st into 3rd ch of turning chain at start of round.

Round 8 Repeat round 7.

Round 9 1 ch to count as 1 dc. 1 dc in each stitch to end of round. Slip stitch into turning chain at start of round.

Round 10 Repeat round 9.

To work the sides
Work four squares as explained (p92) and join together with double crochet joining stitch (chapter 11 for working methods). Sew the squares on to the last round of double crochet of the base.

Round 11 To be worked on to the squares. Repeat round 7.

Rounds 12 to 15 Repeat round 7.
Work the two draw strings finished with a tassel to gather in the top of the bag – (chapter 11 for working methods).

Evening skirt

colour illustration page 51

12×25gm balls of 4–ply yarn in main colour – black (colour A).

10×25gm balls of 4–ply yarn in colour D – green.

6×25gm balls of 4–ply yarn in colour C – royal.

4×25gm balls of 4–ply yarn in colour B – pale blue.

Number 2·50 ISR crochet hook.

Tension one square measures approximately 4in (5cm).

This skirt will fit the average size 12 figure.

Work 108 squares as explained (p92).

Sew together 12 squares to give 9 strips. Sew strips together.

The waistband is worked in the main colour – black.

Join black yarn on edge of one square. Work 5 ch to count as one triple treble stitch, * 1 ch. Miss 1 st, 1 tr tr into next stitch. * Repeat from * to * to complete the top edge of skirt, ending with 1 ch. Miss 1 st, sl st into 5th ch at start of round.

Matching elastic is then threaded through the triple trebles, making the measurement fit your waist.

To work a square

illustrated in the long skirt – colour illustration p51

Four colours are used for this square – A, B, C, D.

Colour A. Work 5 ch. Join with a sl st to form a circle.

Round 1 2 ch to count as 1 h tr. 15 h tr into the circle. Sl st into the second ch at start of round. Break off colour A and join in colour B.

Round 2 4 ch to count as 1 tr and 1 ch space. * 1 tr into next dc. 1 ch. * Repeat from * to * to end of round. Sl st into 3rd ch at start of round. Break off colour B and join in colour C.

Round 3 Sl st into first ch space. 3 ch. 1 pine st (chapter 7) into same space, 3 ch. * 1 pine st into next space, 3 ch, * repeat from * to * to end of round. 1 sl st into 3rd ch at start of round. Break off colour C and join in colour D.

Round 4 Sl st into next 3 ch space. 3 ch to count as 1 tr. 2 tr into same space. 3 tr into each of the next 2 spaces. (1 tr, 2 d tr, 3 ch, 2 d tr, 1 tr) into next space for the corner shaping, * 3 tr into each of the next 3 spaces. (1 tr, 2 d tr, 3 ch, 2 d tr, 1 tr) into next space. * Repeat from * to * to end of round. Sl st into 3rd chain at start of round. Break off colour D and join in colour A.

Round 5 Work 1 ch to count as 1 dc. Work 1 dc into each st of previous round, with 3 dc into each corner 3 ch space.

figure 159

Crazy patchwork

figure 159

This form of crochet is very free and no set instructions can be given. The more experienced worker may like to experiment with this method using oddments of matching yarns. It is easier than it would appear, and once the technique is understood many exciting fabrics may be created. Select a variety of yarns (usually of equal weight) and a variety of stitches. Fabrics can be built up at random.

Begin with a small square, circle or oblong, in one colour, and work in sections along its sides, slip stitching where necessary. Trebles and half trebles and double crochet are used for the sample illustrated.

When working round a sharp, acute-angled corner, increase by working 2 stitches into one stitch and decrease as required when working round an obtuse angle. It is important to test your work after each row, to see if it will lie completely flat. If necessary be prepared to unpick a small section of your work if it will not do so.

Geometric patchwork crochet (figures 160 and 161) can be worked in two methods.

figure 160

Geometric patchwork 1

Individual shapes can be made, such as squares, oblongs and triangles, and joined together to form a fabric. The shapes can be regular or irregular; all the same or mixed. The shapes should be sewn together, and a light pressing is recommended (see working methods, chapter 11). Care should be taken to use harmonizing colours, textures and weights of yarn. Double crochet stitch is recommended for this type of work.

Triangles make a good shape for geometric patchwork. Two shapes are given:

Shape A – small triangle

Row 1 2 ch. 2 dc in 2nd ch from hook. Turn work.

Row 2 1 ch. 1 dc in 2nd st from hook. 1 dc in each of the next 2 sts. Turn work.

Row 3 1 ch. 1 dc in 2nd st from hook. 1 dc in each of the next 3 sts. Turn work.

Row 4 and all following rows Repeat row 3, increasing the number of dc worked until the row: 1 ch and 1 dc in next 13 sts has been worked.

Fasten off cut ends of yarn.

Note: keep turning chains loose.

Shape B – elongated triangle

Row 1 2 ch. 1 dc in 2nd ch from hook. Turn work.

Row 2 1 ch. 1 dc in 2nd st. 1 dc in next st. Turn work.

Row 3 1 ch. 1 dc in 2nd st. 1 dc in next 2 sts. Turn work.

Row 4 1 ch in 2nd st. 1 dc in next 3 sts. Turn work.

Row 5 1 ch in 3rd st. 1 dc in next 4 sts. Turn work.

96

Repeat last row once more.

Continue in dc increasing one st at both ends of the next row, and every following 3rd row until 15 dc are worked.

Fasten off cut ends of yarn.

Note: keep turning chains loose.

These triangles can be worked in two colours and joined together alternately to give a zig-zag effect. Strips of triangles can then be joined to form a fabric (figure 160).

Jacket using this technique

colour illustration p71

Use contrasting shades of Paton's 4-ply yarn and a number 3·00 ISR crochet hook, work strips of crochet fabric using both the triangle shapes explained. As the strips are worked, place them onto your calico pattern (exclude the seam allowance if this is included), until the back pattern and the two front sections are complete. Leave a 3cm border free on both centre front edges and round the neck. The sleeve is made in one piece with the body sections.

Join the strips together using the dc method explained in chapter 11 p102. Additional rows of dc can be added to give any extra shaping. Join together by sewing (see chapter 11) the shoulder seams and side seams. Work the border to centre front edges by working 8 rows in dc. Work a border and ties round the neck to match the centre front borders. The ties are worked over a foundation of 90 chain.

Geometric patchwork 2

Patchwork can also be worked in one piece, using equal weights of yarn. The most suitable stitch to use is double crochet. Designs can be charted on squared paper using two or more colours. Work one stitch for each square on your chart. There is a special method of joining in a new colour of yarn, shown in chapter 11 (p102).

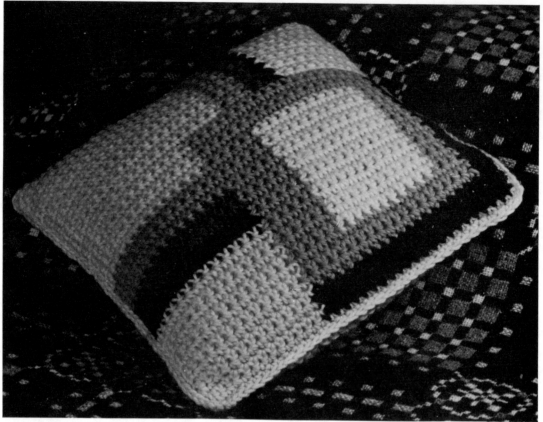

figure 161

Cushion figure 161

2×50gm balls of Paton's Capstan yarn and
oddments of the same yarn in contrasting
colours are used for this cushion. Number 5·00
ISR crochet hook is used.

Tension 6 sts and 7 rows in double crochet to 2in
(5cm).

Work in dc throughout, over 36 sts. The main
colour is natural and the 3 contrasting colours
are introduced as indicated (figure 162). Both
sides can be worked to the same design. When
both sides are complete, place wrong sides
together and join three sides with dc stitch
(chapter 11). Insert cushion pad, and complete
the fourth side.

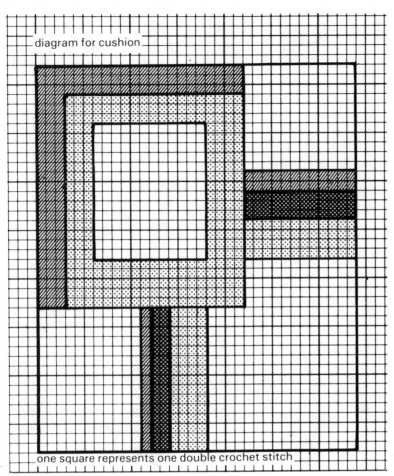

diagram for cushion

one square represents one double crochet stitch

figure 162

11 Working methods

This chapter covers some of the additional finishing techniques required during the working and making up of the various articles explained in this book. Helpful hints are also mentioned to help the reader with any difficulties when reading commercial patterns.

Reading patterns

Throughout this book care has been given to state clearly the number of chain stitches required to start a piece of work. On all following rows additional chains are required as 'turning chains' to count as the first stitch of the row, and these are always quoted at the start of the row. The chart (p23) illustrates clearly these details and should be kept to hand for reference.

Counting stitches When starting a piece of work, always count the number of stitches worked during the last row before starting the next row. The loop on your hook is not counted as a stitch. The turning chain should be included and counts as one stitch of your pattern.

Star/asterisk * . . . . * Indicates a repeat. There are usually two stars and the worker should repeat the instructions between the stars until the end of a row or round. Therefore when you come to the second star, you go back to the first star and repeat the instructions again until you have completed the row. Sometimes the pattern will say, repeat from * to * so many

times more. Then you repeat the instructions by the number stated.

Brackets (. . . . .) Where instructions in brackets are followed by a number, this indicates the number of times the instructions are to be worked. Simply work the instructions by the number stated after the brackets.

Tension

It is important at this stage to mention tension. This is the method of estimating the tightness or closeness of the stitches and it is vital that the tension is correct when working to a set pattern size. However, many of the articles mentioned at the start of this book do not rely wholly on correctness of tension for their success.

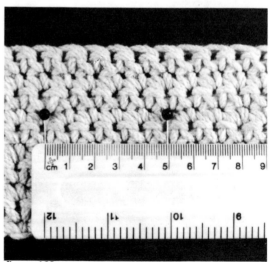

figure 163

Figure 1 (p14) illustrates the usual hook size for the standard yarn types which give an acceptable tension.

To check tension: work a 6in (15cm) square using the hook and yarn stated in the instructions. On this square count the stitches over a 2in (5cm) measure, if too many stitches occur the tension is too tight and the worker should change to a larger hook size. If too few stitches occur, the tension is too loose and the worker should change to a smaller hook size.

Figure 163 illustrates a stitch tension of 5 dc to 2in (5cm).

Figure 164 illustrates 7 rows to 2in (5cm).

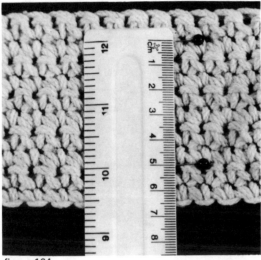

figure 164

Pressing

Always read the manufacturer's instructions on the yarn label regarding heat settings for ironing. Most natural fibre yarns, such as wool and cotton, can be pressed but the man-made yarns need more care, and probably only a very cool iron. Most crochet is most effective if it reveals its textural qualities, and heavy pressing is to be avoided. The exception to this is the seams which, after joining, can often be improved by a *light* pressing always using a pressing cloth over your work. A piece of old towelling makes a good pressing cloth.

Blocking

This is a technique of treating a piece of crochet to give it a definite shape and measurement. Most pieces benefit from blocking.

To block a piece of work: take a firm surface, such as an ironing board if the work is not too large (or a well protected kitchen table will make a good substitute), and cover with an old clean blanket or towel. Cover this padding with a clean sheet and mark out on the sheet the exact measurements required for the article. On to this marked area, pin the work using rustless pins, with the wrong side facing upwards, along the marked position. Cover with a warm, damp cloth, and leave until completely dry. This may take one or two days, depending on the room temperature.

Joining your work

There are basically two ways of joining: (a) sewing, and (b) crochet stitches.

All work should be pressed or blocked before joining.

Sewing Place the two pieces of crochet with right sides together, and pin with safety pins to make sure the pieces fit correctly, matching any stripes. Using a blunt tapestry needle and matching yarn, oversew the two pieces together. Secure the beginning and end of the seam firmly.

Crochet stitches Place the two pieces of crochet with the wrong sides together. Pin with safety pins, matching as before. Make a slip loop with matching or contrasting yarn on your hook, remove hook from loop. Beginning from the right-hand side, to work from right to left, insert hook under two loops of crochet from both pieces of work, pick up slip loop and draw through work. Yoh and draw through loop on hook. ★ Insert hook under two loops of crochet from both pieces of work, one stitch space along seam, yoh and draw through loop. Yoh and draw through both loops on hook. ★ Repeat from ★ to ★ to end of seam. Secure cut ends of yarn firmly. This method of joining can form a definite feature of your design.

Cord stitch (figure 73; p34) can be used the same way as above, working in double crochet from left to right. The skirt in the colour illustration (p51) is joined with cord stitch, the edges of each section first being neatened with a single row of double crochet.

Joining yarn

When joining yarn – same colour – always try to join yarn at the start of a new row; the ends can then be easily sewn into the seam and will not spoil the overall effect. If joins appear during a row, simply leave a length of the old yarn 4in (10cm) long and take up the new yarn, leaving a similar length. Complete your row, and darn the cut ends of yarn into the wrong side of work. Using this method a bumpy knot is avoided.

Joining yarn when working in different colours When working a fabric using colours, care should be taken when joining in the new colour (see **patchwork cushion, figure 161**). The new colour should be placed into the stitch preceeding the stitches to be worked in this colour (figures 165 and 166). The yarn not in use is held behind your work on the wrong side until you reach the position where it is to be used again.

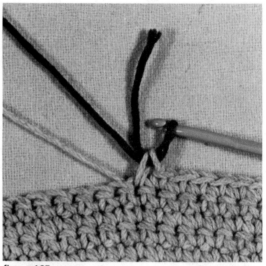

figure 165

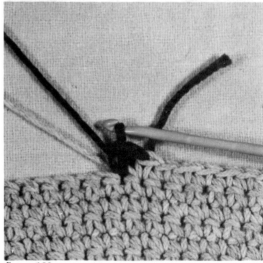

figure 166

figure 167

figure 168

Some finishing touches

Cords Cords are mentioned in the making up of various bags in this book. Cords may be made of crochet or twisted lengths of yarn. Crochet cords are made using the double chain method (chapter 2). Twisted cords are made by taking a number of yarn lengths to give half the desired thickness; twist the yarn lengths in a clockwise direction. When tightly twisted, halve the length and allow the cords to twist back on themselves. To estimate the yarn length required, allow three times the required length of finished cord for twisting.

Figure 167 illustrates three lengths of yarn twisted together to give a six-yarn cord. The cord secures the tassel.

Tassels Tassels form an attractive finishing touch to many bags and cushions illustrated in this book. Small tassels can be made by cutting several lengths of yarn, 4in (10cm) long, and securing with the cord in the centre. Tie together the tassel cords by wrapping yarn several times around the cut pieces. Pull the yarn end through by tying the yarn as shown (figure 167). Note the use of a *sling*. The looped, contrasting yarn is used to pull the tying yarn down into the tassel and is called a sling – it falls away when the yarn is pulled tightly and is of no further use.

Crochet tassel (figure 168) Cut 40 lengths of yarn 15¾in (40cm) long. Fold in half and tie firmly together in the centre with another length of double yarn – approximately 24in (61cm) long – to form the securing yarn of the tassel.

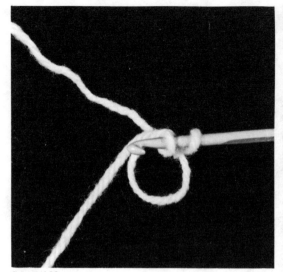

figure 169

figure 170

To work the head of the tassel: wind the yarn round to form a circle ½in (1·25cm) in diameter. Into the circle work 12 dc (figures 169 and 170). Place the securing yarn of tassel through the circle and continue to work in circles with the tassel ends towards you. Work (1 dc into next st. 2 dc into next st) 6 times. Continue in dc until 9 rounds have been completed (figure 171). Fasten off last stitch, and leave a 10in (25cm) length of yarn. Thread cut end of yarn through each dc of last row, tighten and secure. Trim ends of tassel to an even length.

To secure to cushion (figure 168) The double length of securing yarn is drawn through the centre of the circle on cushion ends and tied firmly together. Draw the ends through into the tassel and trim to the same length as tassel ends.

figure 171

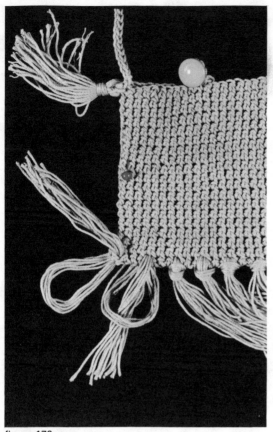

figure 172

figure 173

Fringes Looped-in fringing is an easy and attractive finish to many articles. The bags illustrated in this book are often finished with a fringe along the lower edge or seam. The floor coverings illustrated in the following chapter are also trimmed with a *looped-in* fringe.

Cut lengths of yarn, twice the required fringe depth, and loop through the crochet stitch formed on the edge of your work. Figure 172 illustrates such a fringe being worked on to a little purse. Several lengths of yarn form this fringe.

Figure 173 illustrates a large decorative tassel made to hold back a heavy curtain. The same method is used for making this tassel as described on page 103 with a two–tone twisted cord to form the tie. Two brass hooks hold the cord behind the curtain.

Designing your own fashion outfits

Crochet lends itself particularly well to fashion clothing of all types, from simple stoles and scarves to blouses and full-length jackets and capes. The work grows very quickly and is therefore particularly satisfying. There are no rules as to direction – you can work from side to side, up and down, diagonally, or even in circles. Also, because of the nature of the techniques, a large variety of yarns can be used, giving tremendous scope in colour and texture. Many of the stitches and techniques will have been mastered by now and you should be ready to start your own ideas.

For your first design, select a simple garment of basic shape and let your crochet be the fashion feature. Before starting, choose the yarns and work several samples of crochet in order to select the stitch, colour and hook size. Remember that crochet can be heavy and if you decide to make a long garment the weight must be considered. Heavy yarns used for large areas of work will drag the garment down and elongate the basic shape. Be sure to check your methods of increasing and decreasing so that you can work a shaped edge.

When you have chosen your garment, select a commercial paper pattern, with a minimum number of pattern pieces and no darts. Choose a size of slightly tighter fit than usual because crochet tends to stretch. Cut off the indicated seam allowances and hem turn-up and work your crochet to fit over the paper shape *exactly*, checking your work at very regular intervals. Should you wish to test the pattern first in a calico fabric, a seam allowance of approximately ²/sin (1cm) should be allowed but the crochet will then be worked excluding the seam allowance. You may begin your crochet from any point, from the middle, top or bottom, and work in the required direction until the shape is complete, decreasing and increasing where shaping is required.

For your first experiment it is advisable to work completely in one yarn type and one stitch, eg double crochet or treble stitch. Select yarns of similar weight if mixing yarn colours, as this will give a more balanced fabric. When you are more experienced, different textures and effects can be achieved by using different yarn types and weights.

When you have completed all the pieces of your work, each crochet shape should be blocked very carefully. When the work is thoroughly dry, each piece may be sewn together. The seams may require a very light pressing.

Most of the fashion outfits illustrated in this book were made from a basic paper shape, as explained above. The shape was tested in calico for fitting and the calico *toile* was then used as the pattern for the crochet fabric.

12 Experimental crochet

In this chapter various experimental techniques are illustrated. These techniques could be used for the more decorative and visual applications of crochet, such as wall hangings, three dimensional crochet, and various fashion garments and accessories. Some of the techniques have been used to create floor coverings and fashion articles.

Rag rugs figure 174

Material such as fine woven or knitted-type jersey, made of wool or man-made fibres, is the best to use for this technique. The material should be cut in strips, so preferably select a fabric which does not fray too badly, and cut it into ¾in (2cm) strips. The strips should be continuous and figure 175 (p108) illustrates a quick method of cutting fabric into a continuous length.

Various colours can be used, but one colour has been used for this sample. The rug illustrated is made by working in double crochet throughout using a large hook size, eg number 9·00 ISR depending on the thickness of the material strips. The texture of the double crochet should

figure 174

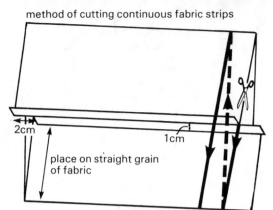

method of cutting continuous fabric strips

2cm

1cm

place on straight grain
of fabric

heavier line = cutting line

place right sides of fabric together and machine
1 cm away from raw edge;   allow 2 cm over hang
at start of seam. Press seam open and cut strips.

figure 175

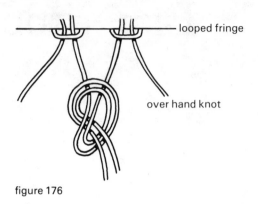

looped fringe

over hand knot

figure 176

be really firm and close. The rug shows a fringed
edge made of string. This is looped into the edge
of the crochet (chapter 11, p105), and an overhand
knot is tied, dividing the fringe lengths from
each loop to form the knot.

Figure 176 shows the working of an overhand
knot.

Rag rug with pile effect

figure 177

This is an unusual and quick technique for
making a rag rug with a pile surface. The same
technique could, of course, be used for other
articles or sections in garments. Strips of fabric
5½in (14cm) × 1in (2·5cm) are used with a string
base. Select a fabric which does not fray too
easily for the best results. Several cut lengths of
yarn could be substituted for the fabric strip and
would make a good fabric for a *mock fur* jacket.

Plain or coloured effects can be achieved, but
one fabric type has been used in this sample for
clarity.

Using a fine string and a number 3·50 ISR
crochet hook, work a foundation chain length
the required size. Work 2 rows in double crochet
to form a firm border.

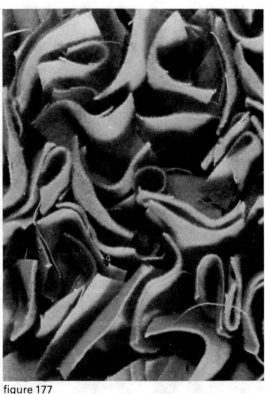

figure 177

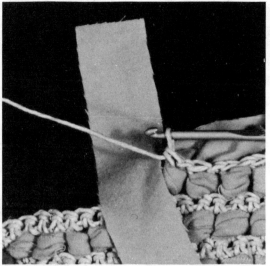

figure 178

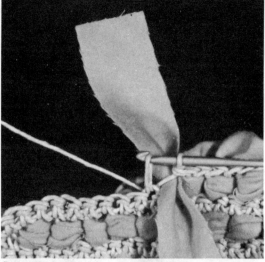

figure 179

Row 1 Work the pile with the wrong side of the work facing you.

2 ch to count as first stitch. 1 h tr in 4th stitch from hook. ★ Place fabric strip over work, next to last stitch worked (figure 178). Insert hook into next stitch, yoh and draw through yarn (figure 179). Place fabric strip which is on wrong side, over and across strip on right side, yoh (figure 180) and draw through both loops on hook. Both ends of the strip should be placed on the right side now, miss 1 dc. 1 ch. ★ Repeat from ★ to ★ to last 2 sts. 1 h tr in each st. Turn work.

Row 2 1 ch to count as 1 dc. 1 dc into 3rd st from hook. 1 dc in each st to end. Turn work.

Repeat rows 1 and 2 throughout.

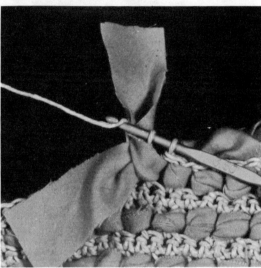

figure 180

figure 181

Crochet over string or cord

Double crochet stitch can be worked over string or cord, or several thicknesses of the working yarn. Using this technique the cord forms a core which gives the fabric a very firm and strong feel. This fabric will not stretch or pull out of shape as readily as crochet worked without such a core. Bases for indoor boots/shoes/socks and bags can be made using this technique. Continuous lengths, or circles can be worked over a core.

To work over cord Work in double crochet. Place the string or cord to form the core behind your working stitch, draw the yarn through the stitch of the previous row in the usual way, yoh (the core will be *between* the loops on the hook and the yarn just picked up) (figure 181) and draw through both loops on hook. Repeat throughout.

figure 182

Rug **figure 182**

This is made in baler twine using this technique –
four lengths of baler twine form the core and
double crochet stitch is worked over the twine.
The ends of the core form an attractive fringed
edging.

Belt **figure 183**

This belt is made of small circles using the same
method. Thirteen circles are made in double
crochet with a chunky knit yarn of matching
colour forming the core. Toning yarns in
Twilley's Lyscordet range were used with a
number 3·00 ISR crochet hook. A surface chain
stitch is worked between the rows of double
crochet and the edge is worked in corded stitch.
A cord and tassel form the tie of this belt.

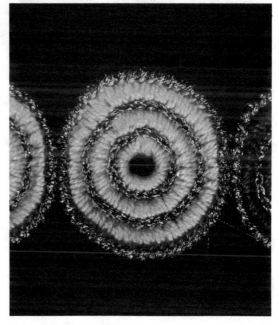

figure 183

Crochet over layers of yarn to form a circle

Double crochet stitch can also be worked over several layers of the working yarn, formed into a circle, or a firm base such as a curtain ring. The crochet stitch is worked in the same manner as for working over a single cord – the ring forming the core for a firm base.

Belt

The colour illustration (p52) shows a belt made of 23 rings using several colours of mohair yarn. Ribbon is threaded through the circles and a commercial buckle completes the fastening.

Bolero

The colour illustration (p72) shows a bolero. Individual circles are worked and placed on to a calico pattern. A seam allowance is shown on the calico and is, of course, omitted in the crochet. When all the necessary area is covered, excluding the darts, each circle is neatly sewn together to form a fabric. The darts are also sewn together.

Figure 184 illustrates a selection of the circles worked for this bolero showing various fillings.

Figure 185 illustrates the positioning of the circles on the calico bolero pattern ready for sewing. The circles come to the edge of the fitting line – the seam allowance is not covered with circles nor is the dart.

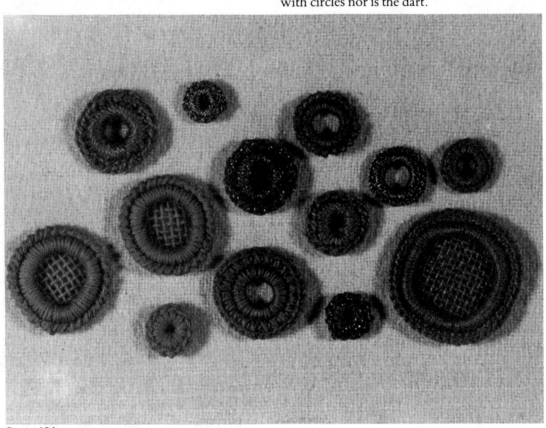

figure 184

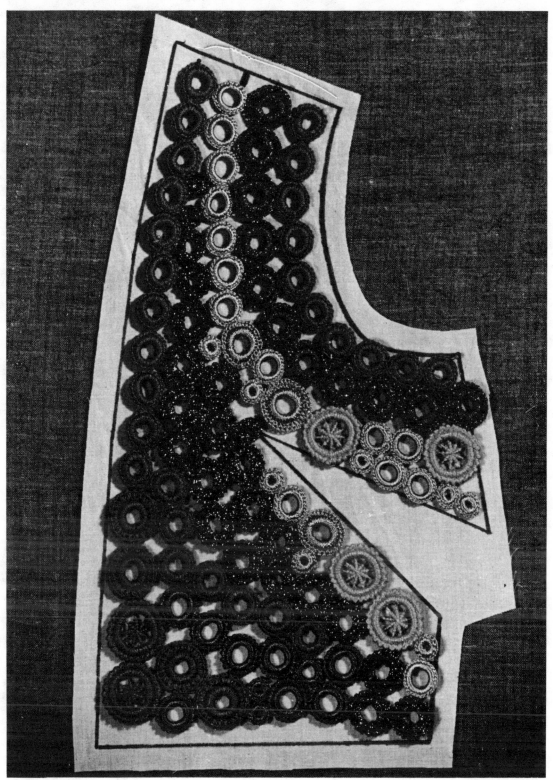

figure 185

figure 186

Crochet over
a string mesh

ie surface double crochet stitch– figure 186

Using a fine string and a number 3·50 ISR
crochet hook, make a chain foundation the
required length. Work 1 row in double crochet
to give a firm edge. Work in double crochet
mesh as used for 'cut fur' fabric (p71) for the
required rug size. End with one double crochet
row to give the firm edge again.

To work the surface stitch Make a slip loop on the
hook. Remove hook, and insert it into the first
space on first mesh row with right side
uppermost. Pick up the slip loop. ★ Insert hook
into *same* space, yoh and draw through yarn,
insert hook into next space, yoh (figure 187) and
draw through both loops on hook. ★ Repeat
from ★ to ★ to end of row. Fasten off stitch on
hook. Break off yarn.

114

Repeat this surface stitch along each row,
beginning from the same side each time. The cut
ends can be left to form a fringe, and should be
trimmed to an equal length.

figure 187

Crochet using leather pieces

Leather shapes, such as squares, oblongs and circles can also be used for a patchwork effect. Leather is an ideal material because it does not fray. The various shapes should be cut out with sharp scissors to give a smooth edge, and holes made around the edge. Mark on the wrong side, $^2/_5$in (1cm) in from the cut edge, and $^2/_5$in (1cm) apart (figure 188). Other non-fraying fabrics can be used, such as PVC and felt. If working with either of these, a piece of heavyweight Vilene should also be placed behind the fabric, or alternatively, the PVC or felt should be used double thickness.

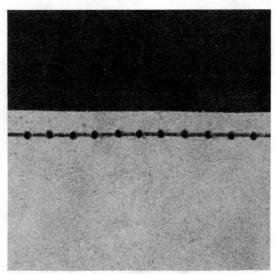

figure 188

To crochet round the edges Make a slip loop on the hook using an appropriate hook size and yarn to fit through the holes made in the leather. Remove hook and, holding the leather with right side facing, work from the right–hand edge. Insert hook into first hole, and draw through the slip loop. Yoh and draw through loop on hook. 1 ch. ★ Insert hook into next hole, yoh and draw through yarn, yoh and draw through both loops on hook. 1 ch. ★ Repeat from ★ to ★ into each hole. Fasten off stitch on hook and break off yarn (figure 189).

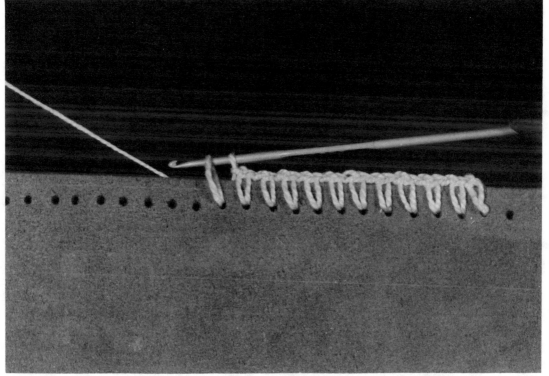

figure 189

figure 190

To join the pieces together Make a slip loop on the hook using a matching or contrasting yarn. Remove hook. Place wrong sides of shapes together, and working from the right-hand edge, place hook through *both* crochet loops of *both* shapes, draw through slip loop, yoh and draw through loop on hook, ★ insert hook into next pair of stitches, yoh and draw through yarn, yoh and draw through both loops on hook, miss next pair of ch sts. ★ Repeat from ★ to ★ to end of seam (figure 190).

Gold leather belt

figure 191

This belt is made of circles of double leather, worked with crochet edges and each circle sewn together to form a length. A cord tie fastens the belt in the front. This technique could also be used for the bolero illustrated earlier in this chapter.

Leather bag figure 190

The bag is made using differing shapes of toning leather, a strip side gusset and a plain back section to match the front. This example uses commercial handles at the opening.

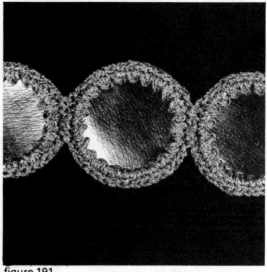
figure 191

Surface crochet – chain stitch

Attractive additions can be made to a plain crochet fabric such as double crochet, by working various designs and motifs on the surface.

The colour illustration (p69) shows a simple two-tone jumper which has been decorated with surface chain stitching.

figure 192

To work the surface chain stitch Work from right side of fabric. Insert hook at edge of work (starting point of your design) and draw through a slip loop. ★ Insert hook into another space, above or beside according to the direction of your design, and draw yarn through fabric (figure 192) *and* through loop on hook. ★ Repeat from ★ to ★ to give the desired lined effect.

Matching yarns or contrasting yarns can be used.

117

Tote bag figure 193

This simple Aran-type tote bag is made using natural coloured Aran yarn (Paton's) and a contrasting colour to form the decorative chain stitching, fringe and cord.

figure 193

Index

accordion stitch, 73–4, 75
asterisks, 100

bags, 40, 41, 54
  beach, 60
  evening, 82, 92, 93
  leather, 117
  tote, 30, 118
  vegetable, 61
baler twine, 111
beach bag, 60
belts, 20, 83, 111, 112, 117
blocking, 101, 106
block stitch, 68
bobble stitch, 66
bolero, 112
boots, house, 82
brackets, 100
broom-handle stitch, 45
bullion stitch, 53

calico toile, 75, 97, 106
chain fur stitch, 66
chain lace, 55, 61
chain stitch, 17
  surface, 117
charts, designing, 87, 88, 89
check stitch, 42, 54
chevron stitch, 76, 77
choker, 35
circles, 23, 55, 73, 90–1, 111, 112
cluster stitch, 69
coat, 75
cord, 20, 29, 30, 103, 110
cord stitch, 34, 111
counterpane stitch, 36, 40
counting stitches, 100
crazy patchwork, 95
crossed double trebles, 44
crossed trebles, 57, 60

cushions, 54, 68, 73, 98
cut fur stitch, 67

decreasing, 32, 33
designing, 106
  charts, 87, 88, 89
double chain stitch, 19
double crochet stitch, 21, 23
  ridged, 37
double treble stitch, 23, 28
  crossed, 44
  raised crossed, 39

ending work, 18
equipment, 13, 14
evening bag, 82, 92, 93
evening skirt, 94

fabrics, 90
filet crochet, 84
filet mesh, 86, 87, 88
filet stitch, 85
flower motifs, 88, 89
foundation chain, 16, 17, 18, 19, 22, 23
fringes, 30, 62, 89, 105, 108

geometric patchwork, 96, 97

half treble stitch, 23, 24
hat, 62, 75
hook size, 13, 14, 15, 18
horizontal trebles, 48
house boots, 82

increasing, 31, 32–3
ironing, see pressing

jacket, 82, 97
joining leather, 116
joining work, 102

joining yarn, 102
jumper, 82

knot, 108

leather, 115
  bag, 117
  belt, 117
  joining, 116
  sole, 82
leg warmers, 82
loop stitch, 64
  multiple, 74, 75
looped chain, 58

material, *see* yarn
multiple loop stitch, 74, 75

neatening edges, 34
neck purses, 29

one-way crochet, 23, 38, 39, 42, 44, 45, 47, 48, 53, 64
one-way star stitch, 47

patchwork
  crazy, 95
  geometric, 96, 97
patterns, 23, 80, 100
  paper, 106
pine stitch, 69
popcorn stitch, 67
pressing, 101, 106
purses, 29

quadruple treble stitch, 23, 29

rag rugs, 107, 108–9
raised trebles, 38, 39, 41
raised crossed double trebles, 39, 41
reversible crochet, 24, 36, 37, 38, 43, 44, 46, 48
ridged double crochet, 37, 40
rug, 111
  rag, 107, 108–9

scarf, 30, 62, 75, 89
shawl, 88
shell stitch, 48
skirt, evening, 94
slip loop, 16

slip stitch, 18, 23
Solomon's knot stitch, 59, 62
spaced trebles, 56, 60
squares, 90, 92, 94
star stitch, 46
  one-way, 47
stars, 100
step stitch, 43
stitches
  advance, 42
  open, 55
  primary, 15
  see also individual stitches
stole, 62
string, 61, 110, 114
  mesh, 114
stripes, 79
surface chain stitch, 117
surface zig zag stitch, 44

tassels, 29, 30, 46, 93, 103–4, 105
tension, 100
textures, 64
thread, *see* yarn
three-colour patterns, 80
toile, calico, 75, 97, 106
tote bag, 30
treble stitch, 23, 26, 58, 75
  crossed, 57, 60
  horizontal, 48
  raised, 38, 41
  spaced, 56, 60
trebles in relief, 37, 40, 45
triangles, 96
triple trebles, 23, 28
turning chains, 21, 22, 23, 24
twine, baler, 111
two-colour fabric, 80, 81

vegetable bag, 61

waistcoat, 75
working methods, 100
woven fabrics, 79, 83

yarn, 13, 14, 55, 101, 102, 106, 112
yarn over hook, 17

zigzag stitch, 77–8